*Competition is Killing Us*

ABOUT THE AUTHOR

Michelle Meagher is a Senior Policy Fellow at the University College London Centre for Law, Economics and Society and co-founder of the Inclusive Competition Forum, a think tank focused on democratizing corporate power and the enforcement of competition law. Michelle is a UK- and US-qualified lawyer, specializing in competition law and corporate governance. Michelle sits on the corporate governance committee of the Institute of Chartered Accountants in England and Wales.

# Competition is Killing Us

*How Big Business is Harming Our Society
and Planet – and What to Do About It*

## MICHELLE MEAGHER

**BUSINESS**

PENGUIN BUSINESS

UK | USA | Canada | Ireland | Australia
India | New Zealand | South Africa

Penguin Business is part of the Penguin Random House group of companies
whose addresses can be found at global.penguinrandomhouse.com.

First published 2020
001

Typeset in 11/13 pt Dante MT Std
Typeset by Integra Software Services Pvt. Ltd, Pondicherry
Printed and bound in Great Britain by Clays Ltd, Elcograf S.p.A.

A CIP catalogue record for this book is available from the British Library

ISBN: 978-0-241-42301-1

Follow us on LinkedIn: https://www.linkedin.com/company/penguin-connect/

www.greenpenguin.co.uk

Penguin Random House is committed to a
sustainable future for our business, our readers
and our planet. This book is made from Forest
Stewardship Council® certified paper.

For Indigo, Malachi and Dan,
who show me daily what life is really about

# Contents

# Contents

# Contents

# Preface: Changing my mind about the free market

It was a spring day like any other for the 4 million people working in the 3,000 textile factories spread across the heaving mega-city of Dhaka, Bangladesh, the fourth largest urban metropolis in the world. Workers made their way from crowded bedrooms into crowded streets, on to crowded rickshaws, down crowded alleys and into crowded workshops, weaving their way through the noisy thoroughfares strewn with discarded rubbish. They took up their places at sewing machines and assembly lines, to earn their 32 US cents an hour, no different from workers starting their day in workplaces all over the world.

Except that on that day, 24 April 2013, one of those workplaces, the complex of makeshift factories that was known as Rana Plaza, collapsed, killing 1,134 people. It turned out that some of those workers were as young as thirteen years old. A further 2,500 people were injured and had to be rescued from the rubble, some regaining consciousness only weeks later. It was the deadliest structural failure in human history.

The story soon emerged that dangerous cracks in the building's facade had been reported the day before, and parts of the building had been evacuated. But the seamstresses and machine workers had been ordered to return to work the next day or face dismissal.[1] Cheap jeans, bound for Western markets, will not sew themselves.

On the day that Rana Plaza collapsed, the lives of the surrounding community were changed for ever. The news ricocheted across the world, making headlines in the US, UK and across Europe. Under intense media scrutiny, clothing brands and suppliers frantically tried to establish whether their garments were made in that factory, revealing the awful truth that many of them were not immediately sure either way. But then the global news agenda moved on, and the 'fast fashion' machine – built on a business model of cheap, disposable clothes and cheap, disposable workers – cranked back into gear, with the brands giving only hollow commitments to increase safety.

The Rana Plaza collapse is often labelled an accident, even though it was foreshadowed just a few months before by the Tazreen factory fire in Dhaka, which killed over 100 people. Fashion is considered a competitive industry. If safety standards are not adequately enforced or maintained, if unappealing work and appalling working conditions land in the poorest countries, and if tragedy is the price of productivity, it is no one's fault – no one has the power to do other than what the market allows.

But the commercial pressures that squeeze factory owners, clothing brands, and even the workers and consumers, suggest that the tragedy was not an accident – it was systemically inevitable. The product is not 'clothes', the product is 'cheap clothes', and the business model is simple: outsource manufacturing to the cheapest possible factories, remaining wilfully blind to the real sources of the cost savings. Primark, Matalan, Benetton, Bonmarché – these are high street brands, worn by millions of people in the West. The clothes are cheap but the business is enriching. In fact, the owner of Zara, one of the brands implicated at Rana Plaza, is one of the richest people in the world.[2] If we treat Rana Plaza as an accident, we cannot learn the right lessons and prevent such a disaster from happening again.

We need to see Rana Plaza for what it is: an extreme manifestation of a system designed to value money over human lives, and which does not place enough responsibility on those who could do something about it. Corporations, with the power to push costs on to the public, enriching those who are already wealthy, with businesses that take more than they give back to society, face little in the way of accountability or punishment. It is raw power, embedded within our economic system, which we consistently fail to see. The moment of reckoning never seems to come.

Unless the executives of the companies whose clothes were produced at Rana Plaza happen to have been uniquely sociopathic, we must assume that no human being involved in the chain of decisions and omissions that led to the collapse wanted it to happen. So how did it happen? How did they get away with it? And why, after such a catastrophe, have things not fundamentally changed?

## Career capitalist

For me, the tragedy at Rana Plaza held a personal resonance. Although I have lived most of my life in the UK, I am Bangladeshi by origin and my mother's family comes from Dhanmondi in Dhaka, just fifteen miles from the Savar Upazila district where Rana Plaza sat. My parents rarely tell us stories of home, in an effort, I think, to insulate us from the weight of our history. But with the precious few family legends they do recount, the moral of the story is always the same: my parents uprooted themselves and made a life in a foreign land, thousands of miles removed from their families, traditions and culture, so that their children would never have to suffer the fate of those 1,134 people.

We were raised in the UK, with the opportunity to attend some of the best universities in the world. But, unlike my siblings, I opted not to fulfil my parents' wishes to save lives, one by one, by becoming a doctor. No, I would save them en masse by becoming a competition lawyer, spreading freer and more efficient markets around the world with every legal submission and brief.

Competition law – or 'antitrust', as it is called in the US – is about maintaining fair competition in undistorted markets. Free markets, I believed, were the key to delivering education, healthcare, democracy, peace – and, above all, the flourishing of the human spirit. No profession could be more noble than the one tasked with defending the freedom of the markets. And so I embarked on a degree in Philosophy, Politics and Economics at Oxford University, studied competition law at graduate school at Georgetown, Washington, and went to work for some of the biggest law firms in the world.

Fast-forward ten years into my free market career and I found myself with my eyes glued to the television screen. It is not often that you see so many petite, brown women on every major news channel, but here they were – women who looked just like myself and my sister, except for the saris and salwars, the bindis and betel nuts. And they had been crushed to death by the hazardous building in which they worked. How could such a thing happen in the twenty-first century? Surely this was too terrible a price to pay for free market competition? Was this the benevolent freedom of markets that I, as a competition lawyer, was supposed to be upholding?

## Thirst for truth

Around the same time as the catastrophic Rana Plaza collapse, with these seeds of doubt about free market competition just taking root in my mind, I found myself working day and night on something far less consequential: calculating the respective market shares of two merging fizzy drinks companies – a statistic referred to in the business, rather graphically, as the 'share of throat'.

I had worked on all sorts of cases as a competition lawyer, in all sorts of markets, but somehow it was this fizzy drinks merger that got me. It could have been groceries or banking or memory chips or ready-mix concrete or shipping or waste or trucks or computer screens, all of which I had worked on. But stuck in the office at 3 a.m. in an attempt to meet yet another deadline, I had an epiphany: lowering the price of carbonated sugar water and increasing the output of the company – the primary goal of competition law – would never be good for society.

In that moment, I realized that the idea that companies fixated on a need to deliver maximum returns to shareholders would somehow benefit the public at large through free market competition was completely backwards. It suddenly seemed that trying to make markets fairer, with even more intense competition, was entirely beside the point; it was like carefully packing and pressing a parachute with a great big hole in it.

I saw that an economic system producing more and more stuff was not necessarily better, that free markets are not really free, and fair competition, within such markets, was not really fair.

It was unnerving to discover the inconvenient truths ignored by the free market paradigm, but which had been there all along. Rana Plaza was the loose thread in the fabric of my understanding, but when I started to pull it, the whole thing unravelled: more competitive markets could be harmful; but also, looking closely, it seemed that many, if not most, markets were actually not that competitive. Big, powerful companies abound. How did that happen?

It was as if I had stepped from firm, solid ground into a formless void, outside the framework and enclosure of free market thinking. Growing up, I had been a teenage conservative. My sister even gave me the nickname 'Thatch' for my sympathies with Margaret Thatcher's policies on trade unions and the minimum wage. At one point my favourite book was Ayn Rand's libertarian fantasy of godlike tycoons, *Atlas Shrugged*. I was a true believer in free markets – before and, even more so, after studying economics – and I became a competition lawyer to spread that gospel. I had made my home in the neoliberal consensus.

But by 2013, as I clocked endless billable hours, my doubts were piling up. Having dedicated my whole career to competition, it was confusing for me to contemplate the inadequacy of free markets – toiling to defend a £1.4 billion fizzy drinks merger was not going to make the world a better place.

It is hard to convey how painful the process of completely changing my own world view has been. But in adopting a new perspective I am in good company: Keynes once said, 'When the information changes, I change my mind. What do you do?' What I began to understand, slowly – too slowly, no doubt – was that the information had changed; the old economic models were no longer accurate (if they ever had been).

Competitive markets, it seemed, were extremely effective at consumption and destruction. But efficient? Beneficent? Hardly. I could not sleep for thinking about how to fix this fundamental mistake in the design of the economy. For some people this would have been an academic question, something to ponder with a friend over a glass of wine whilst putting the world to rights or perhaps something to tuck away into a mental folder marked 'Capitalist Contradictions' (because we all have one of those!). For me, it was an existential crisis, so closely had I tied my career and identity to the notion of free markets.

And with that disquiet came a radically different way of thinking about capitalism. I started to wonder if our focus on the benefits of the market – the low prices and plentiful output that we get as consumers – was distracting us from the costs – the pollution and inequality and poor health and powerlessness – that hit us as workers, parents, citizens, and as people living on planet Earth.

I am not a radical person – I am by nature risk averse, if anything – but having caught a glimpse of the world as it really is, there was no going back to wilful ignorance. It was daunting to contemplate all the things that our free market model does not consider. But the time had come for me to question some of my core beliefs and take action to see if markets could be made to be truly fair.

I still believed in the power of the private sector to do good; that business did not have to be bad for our planet and species. I believed that a free society and political democracy could be bolstered by free enterprise and economic democracy. But more competition between profit-hungry firms did not seem to be the complete solution, not even close.

So, I quit my high-flying job at a big law firm and went in search of companies trying to have a positive impact on the world. What I found was a vibrant fringe of businesses operating at the edges of capitalism. They were still competing, but in a completely different way. Instead of existing in opposition to society – seeing what harms they could get away with and how much profit they could amass in the meantime – these businesses were actively trying to serve society, often inviting society into the boardroom to help guide their influential reserves of corporate power and resources. It was free markets, but not at all as I knew it.

## Competition is not what you think it is

What I discovered on my journey was that free market competition is not what it seems to be. We have a growing problem of corporate power in our societies because we have failed to understand how free market competition actually works. Competition does not disperse power, it creates power. Not all competition is good for us.

The insistent mantra of free, competitive markets is a distasteful joke, to which our impoverished planet and society are the unfortunate punchline. This, in itself, is increasingly well understood – at least outside of the mainstream – but amongst the people who could actually change the way things work, this observation generally elicits an exasperated throwing up of hands. *What to do about it?* they ask, fatigued with the repetition. In fact, we already do plenty, and that is half the problem: there is a vast and busy industry of regulators, lawyers, economists, lawmakers, consultants and scholars, nudging companies incessantly, and self-servingly, with a complex system of incentives and punishments. But the net effect is alarmingly deficient.

As someone who positioned themself on the front line of this well-intentioned but wholly inadequate effort to remedy the less palatable tendencies of market capitalism, I had to eventually, and reluctantly, face the reality that we are pushing and prodding markets not nearly hard enough, and often in entirely the wrong direction. I began to fear that the whole exercise was pointless, or worse – a mere distraction from what we should really be doing.

I came to see that the regulatory infrastructure designed to maintain free markets and contain corporate power – antitrust – is a half-hearted, technocratic effort that is simply not working. We are prevented at every turn from taking decisive action by a few pervasive myths about free market competition that keep us in perpetual hope, ignorance and wilful complacency. We are paralysed into cultural and political inertia, even as the economic system charges devastatingly ahead. And we have not developed another way of doing things; there are woefully few alternative narratives for how we can succeed in a capitalist economy.

Competition itself is the creator of power – markets inexorably tend towards concentration, and we seem incapable of enforcing the required level of restraint to prevent the accumulation of money and power. The critical questions that go unasked are: *Creation of power for whom? And at whose expense?*

We hesitate to identify the winners of the race to market dominance as 'monopolists'. We do not want to seem ungrateful or unworldly. We cannot see that the 'competition' that got them to the top is not the same kind of 'competition' that keeps them there. We cannot see that a market, an economy, a society dominated by big companies acting with impunity cannot be competitive. We may all benefit from innovation, productivity, efficiency – if these are, indeed, handmaidens to monopoly (itself a debatable proposition). But it is an absurdly lopsided bargain. Free market competition has become a euphemism for the accumulation of power by the already powerful. And the immeasurable harms of the so-called competitive system proceed under this intellectual cover.

This is a book about power, the power that is embedded in every market interaction and which flows so freely towards those who already have it that we tread the paths it clears in its wake, without realizing that there are other paths not taken. This is a book about the structures of influence, the landscape of leverage and the contours of control. This is a book about who gets to take up space in our societies and for what purpose. This is a book about the economic systems that make a tragedy like Rana Plaza possible, even inevitable, and what we can do about it.

It is with great trepidation, but with a strong and irresistible conviction of spirit, that I seek to expose the myths surrounding free market competition. Other campaigners take on other pieces of the puzzle, the fight is fought on many fronts, and the myths themselves have a tendency to resist challenge. They have become so enmeshed in the capitalist system that the entire economy is coordinated according to their logic. I expect fierce resistance from the many agents of competitive markets – companies, investors, governments, even consumers – for the interlocking nature of the myths operates like a maddening psychological puzzle, whereby shaking yourself free involves burrowing deeper into the matrix. If I am successful in my attempts to disabuse you, dear reader, of what may be some of your most strongly held beliefs, you may experience confusion, disorientation, or disillusionment. Fear not: you will not have me alone for company and encouragement. We are many, seeking new and better answers, and we are not giving up.

# Introduction: Debunking the myths of competition

We live in a time of big companies. Ever since the privilege of forming a company was first granted, there have been private organizations with the power and backing of nations and they have wielded that power across the globe. Now it seems as if an ever-dwindling roster of companies – in Big Food, Big Tech, Big Pharma – have a say in how our economy works and for whom, and the shadow of that influence reaches deep into our personal lives and stretches out before us into the unfolding path of our shared future.

In 2004, when Google went public on the stock market, it was valued at what seemed at the time to be an impossible $23 billion. Ten years later it was worth $390 billion. In 2018 it was worth $766 billion. Amazon is now worth over $1 trillion. There is no need to assume sinister intentions on the part of company founders, executives, investors, lenders, or any of those that stand to benefit financially from the dazzling ascent of our biggest companies, before questioning whether it is right that such capital, power and influence should be concentrated in the hands of so few individuals. Facebook, for example, is technically a publicly owned company, but it is effectively controlled by one human being – Mark Zuckerberg – who has the deciding vote on all decisions made by one of the biggest and most powerful companies in the world.

Free markets are, in theory, constrained by democratic process. But where is the economic democracy capable of holding the unfathomable power of today's industry titans to account? The answer is: *There is very little that big companies are not able to do, and we have relinquished the tools that were once designed to enclose them.*

It turns out that we have been systematically ignoring the power that readily accumulates in so-called 'free markets', and this simple oversight is responsible for untold economic grief. We have ended up with rising levels of power held by a few companies in key industries, moulding entire markets in their image. Until we change how these corporations operate, and for whom, our smartphone manufacturers will continue to clear pristine forests in the hunt for precious metals to line consumer gadgets destined for the rubbish heap, and workers will continue to be exploited in the ironically named 'fulfilment centres' of online shopping giants. We do alarmingly little to challenge corporate abuse, deterred by entrenched commercial and intellectual forces that continue to advocate regulatory inertia. The ideas, and the power, calcify, creating a cage from which we have failed to break free, because we are unable even to see that it is there.

## The hidden waste of efficient free markets

Competition is the rivalry between suppliers in the market as they strive to get consumers to buy from them.* Competitive markets are exalted for bringing consumers cheap products, and plenty of them. It seems a small leap to assume that a 'competitive' market is one with lots of suppliers competing – that must be what politicians mean when they say we should have a competitive economy – right? Possibly. As this book will show,

---

* I could not avoid using the word 'competition' in a book about competition, but its meaning is not straightforward. Please refer to the Glossary at the back of the book for guidance on this and other troublesome words used throughout this book.

'competition' is often in the eye of the beholder: it can mean many small rivals competing, or it can mean a few companies in fierce contest; it can mean a market with lots of choices, or it can mean one company heralded as the most 'competitive' of all (generally this is the competitiveness politicians have in mind). We can all agree that competition is good precisely because we all mean different things by it.

What is vitally important, but often overlooked when we glorify competition, is that it matters what exactly companies are competing for. In a free market, companies are free to pursue power and profits in ways that harm society and the planet. Uber is able to under-provide worker protections for drivers and grow exponentially by trampling over local regulations; meanwhile society pays for the social safety net that Uber does not itself supply. Social media companies build a business model of 'free' products commercialized through surveillance and data extraction, but when a democratic election is subverted it affects even those who do not use the platforms – the effects spill out into the wider world. Global banks are able to take risks for which we all must pay the price when the entire financial system is brought to the brink of collapse. Energy companies can conceal the true cost of burning fossil fuels until the problem is so widespread and their activities are so systemically important that we are paralysed into inaction – even when faced with the extinction of our own species. And clothing retailers are allowed to turn a blind eye to the conditions in their supply chains, enabling them to keep costs down with this delinquency.

These social and environmental costs that are not accounted for in the market transactions that generate them are what economists call 'externalities', and it is easy to see that a free market will produce many such costs – too many – as, by definition, no one in particular is held accountable for them.

But externalities are not accidents. Creating negative spillovers is what many companies, programmed to maximize returns for shareholders, are implicitly designed to do. The parallel tyranny of consumers and shareholders gives rise to repellent breaches of sound economic or ecosystem organization in favour of corporate interests and the accumulation of corporate power, all in the name of competition.

Competition, and the faith we place in competition to benefit us all and to disperse power throughout the economy, is the critical blind spot that lies unexamined within capitalist doctrine, and it looms large in our economic policy, an elephant that completely crowds out everything else in the room. It is the plot twist in our free market story, laid bare by Rana Plaza – the collapsed building and the pile of bodies. It is a truth sitting buried underneath the neoliberal monolith that has come to circumscribe all that is relevant to public policy.

We have steadfastly ignored the reality of corporate power, especially when it comes to regulating big companies. It even feels like a betrayal of free market ideology to single out big corporations – there is something unsophisticated about failing to appreciate the benefits of bigness when everyone knows that globe-spanning multinationals are more efficient than local businesses, don't they? But this terra incognita is exactly where we must step if we are to gain purchase on the crises that threaten our society and planet. Nothing should be taken for granted – even, or especially, the role of the most significant and substantial actors in the industries over which they claim their dominion.

## *Free market myths*

One blind spot – so how hard can it be to see clearly past it? Extremely hard.

As I found out when I opened Pandora's box, behind that one blind spot sit six free market myths that urge us to reconsider

4

any attempt to recalibrate free market competition. One or more of these myths is at play whenever free market logic is called into question, and the myth usually wins.

So here they are, six commonly accepted myths which, as we shall see, have roots in eighteenth-century economic thinking, laid out and ready for a fresh evaluation in the cold, hard light of the twenty-first century.

## Six myths of free market competition

- Myth #1: Free markets are competitive.
- Myth #2: Companies compete by trying to best respond to the needs of society.
- Myth #3: Corporate power is benign.
- Myth #4: We already control corporate power with antitrust.
- Myth #5: The law requires companies to maximize financial value for shareholders.
- Myth #6: We are all shareholders; we all benefit from corporate focus on shareholders' interests.

Remarkably, these myths – mere stories about how the economy might theoretically work – have been enshrined in the law and in business practice. And the flipside of these arguments – that government and society are inefficient, wasteful, bureaucratic and not innovative – becomes the justification for non-intervention in the market.

In this book we will take each of these myths in turn to reveal the reality that is currently being obscured. Free market competition does not disperse power, it creates power. In fact 'competition' has come to be synonymous with market domination. Companies compete for power, for the benefit of their shareholders, in ways that harm society. There are many types of corporate power that allow the powerful to choose how to shape the economy and society in their interests. Modern

5

antitrust does little to constrain corporate power and, instead, condones it. Corporate directors need not maximize shareholder returns – the law is being wilfully misinterpreted to our collective detriment. This is doubly damaging because most shareholders are already wealthy.

There have been many attempts to debunk the principles of 'neoliberalism' – the overarching ideology that these myths serve to reinforce. The challenge is to do something with the insight that things do not need to be – and should not be – this way. We need to act on the knowledge that we are being governed by a defunct system of beliefs that is driving us off a cliff. In this book I will engage with ideas about how to change the regulation of corporate power – how to acknowledge power in all its guises, to restrain excessive corporate power and to redistribute the remaining power more equally across society.

What has become clear is that the unwavering focus on shareholder returns and profit is endangering lives, threatening society and compromising the habitability of our planet. Governments struggle to keep up with an economic system designed to devour the world and every resource within it, and it has taken us longer than it should have to face up to the fact that we are living precariously on a finite, crowded and divided planet that is steadily getting warmer.

The costs of free markets and the true power of companies have been completely removed from our analysis exactly where this would be most relevant – in the discipline of antitrust, which is meant to deliver the vaunted benefits of competition to the masses. Antitrust law is supposed to protect competition, promote market fairness and prevent power from accumulating. But power and externalities have been slowly displaced in antitrust thinking, replaced instead by a single-minded focus on low prices for consumers. Economic democracy is equated with the opportunity to spend, and to buy more and more, even whilst the tragic collapse of our ecosystem is unfolding.

Once we are released from the hypnotic hold of these free market myths, we will be free to reconfigure capitalism in fundamental ways, safe in the knowledge that the alarmist warnings of doom that greet anyone attempting to step beyond neoliberalism are there to serve the interests of the few, not the many.

## Power, power everywhere, and not a drop to drink

These free market myths were inserted into antitrust thinking as the discipline came to be dominated by economics. The result is that competition law, like many other areas of law, has become an increasingly technocratic field. It is now a niche discipline that most people find impenetrable if they have not dedicated their lives to it. And it turns out that this veil of ignorance, which the antitrust community tends to reinforce rather than remove, has done us a collective disservice. Without full public understanding and oversight, antitrust has supervised the grand reshaping of our economic world into what it is today.

Within antitrust, there has been a wholesale shift over the last century from a discussion of power, democracy and the best way to organize a just society, towards a narrow assessment of the economic welfare of prototypical consumers. There is so much that this version of economics leaves out, assumes away, ignores or minimizes, and many of our fears, concerns and vulnerabilities fall between those cracks. We no longer challenge corporate power at its heart by dissolving companies whose corporate abuses subvert the public interest. We have moved from the language of politics and social justice, comprehensible to the lay person, to the vocabulary and formulae of economics, unintelligible even to many of the officials responsible for administering the competition regime.

In the meantime, antitrust practitioners have managed to diligently develop a complicated regulatory framework for market power that somehow allows markets to consolidate anyway. Even more egregiously, we – as a society – have misconstrued the true nature of corporate power itself. We cannot see what is right in front of us. Antitrust's fixation with price, although amenable to economic quantification, will not help us contain power beyond the economist's narrowly construed definition of market power. If we only look at whether prices will go up or down, we cannot capture the many broader, more subtle, surreptitious and insidious ways in which companies can bend the economy and society to their will.

Regulators – antitrust authorities included – have their work cut out for them as the impacts of corporate conduct refuse to limit themselves to national jurisdictional boundaries. With the majority of the world's biggest companies headquartered in America, and with the American regulatory approach historically influential across the world, we must all look to the United States to understand how we arrived at our world of big, unaccountable companies and how we might move forward.

The global community of antitrust lawyers, economists, officials, scholars and practitioners must face up to what has been a profound dereliction of duty. Charged with safeguarding the progress of industrial development, we adopted such a narrow interpretation of our task that we managed to supervise the mass consolidation of industry on the blanket, untested and rather naive assumption that, with the potential for low prices always dangled before our eyes, no harm could come from the rise of colossal companies. It happened on our watch.

Thankfully, times are changing. In 2019, the influential Business Roundtable group of 180 CEOs of America's most powerful companies declared that shareholder value would no longer rule supreme in the boardrooms of their companies – although it remains to be seen whether they really mean it. The Scottish Government, the Welsh Assembly and the UK Parliament each declared a climate emergency. In the US, antitrust authorities have opened investigations into the power of the tech titans, dozens of attorneys general across the United States are bringing cases against Facebook and Google, and presidential candidates Elizabeth Warren and Bernie Sanders have placed antitrust at the top of the agenda, alongside an attempt to create real corporate responsibility for the biggest companies.

But there are two separate conversations happening: about corporate power and monopoly on the one hand, and shareholder value and corporate responsibility on the other. Until we realize that these are actually the same conversation – that corporate power can undermine corporate responsibility and that corporate responsibility is meaningless if companies are slavishly pursuing power – then we will not be able to start the hard work of re-engineering global capitalism for a sustainable, or even survivable, future.

## *Power, interrupted*

How should we react when Amazon makes a move to become the sole platform through which the US government conducts all its tenders for anything from paperclips to power plants? What are the implications when Facebook announces it is creating its own currency? What does it mean when the UK government seeks to introduce more competition into healthcare? Will oil companies be the ones to save us from climate change?

To answer these questions, we must leave eighteenth-, nineteenth- and twentieth-century thinking behind and step bravely and purposefully into the next decades, recalibrating our models for the twenty-first century. After dismantling the six free market myths that perpetuate the major blind spot in our models of free market competition – the failure to perceive the power of corporations and how they can use that power to foist harm on to an unsuspecting and subservient society – we can make space for a new economic logic, enabling us to reclaim corporate power and reinstate public service for big and powerful companies.

## Stakeholder antitrust

This book offers a new vision for corporate power in the economy – directed not by lax antitrust regulation of shareholder value companies but by 'stakeholder antitrust'. At the heart of this vision is a rejection of the idea that free markets naturally respond to the interests of the public. Stakeholders – not just shareholders but workers, communities, governments and the environment – should instead be given an active role in shaping their economic reality.

Stakeholder antitrust consists of two elements.

1. A broader understanding of corporate power and a recognition that, in otherwise 'free' markets, robust antitrust enforcement is needed to constantly constrain the market and to limit the economic and political power of firms
2. A fundamental change in the nature of incorporation for our most powerful companies so that they are governed by and for their stakeholders, with the ultimate penalty for repeated transgression against the public interest being dissolution of the company

Together, these two elements will help to ensure that economic democracy can prevail within market capitalism.

As the devastating risk of climate and societal breakdown looms on the near horizon, the urgency of establishing stakeholder influence over the corporate activities of the largest and most influential companies grows ever stronger. This can be achieved by truly democratizing companies, sharing power within the corporate hierarchy with stakeholders, and creating a platform for stakeholders, not just shareholders, to guide companies in line with the public interest. The tendency of corporate power to accumulate can be challenged through antitrust regulation, but companies should also be forced to use their power in ways that genuinely support the public interest, and there should be ultimate limits placed on the power of companies. At the same time, stakeholders should be given more power to direct corporate activities.

With stakeholder antitrust, we would start this overhaul of the corporate sector in areas where the power is most concentrated and the costs most prolific. Antitrust is therefore key to both identifying power and limiting the possibility that any other regulatory interventions will be undermined. Antitrust should not just be the sleepwalking referee for free market competition, it should be our relentless guard against unwarranted and unchecked corporate power, and we need that now more than ever.

Happily, we have at our disposal a powerful, mobile and flexible tool with which to plug the gaps, a robust social, legal and institutional structure that can corral people and vast resources and direct them towards any chosen end: the corporation. We can regulate the company as a channel through which governments and communities, not just unforgiving global capital, can act for the public good, and we can activate this redesign in the biggest and most powerful companies through antitrust – never once forgetting that the corporation is capable also of devastation and destruction. We are the ones with the responsibility to maintain a firm grip and a wary eye.

Antitrust and corporate law – two arcane spheres of regulation – have failed to contain corporate power over the last century, hamstrung by economic theories that enfeebled them from the inside out. And yet, lying dormant within them, they may uniquely contain the tools for our potential salvation. Antitrust and corporate law can allow us to curb corporate abuse right at the source – within the corporation itself.

We are recognizing the failures of corporate capitalism not a moment too soon, and hopefully not too late. We need big companies to share their power and we, the people of the world, need to reclaim it. And we need to start now.

## PART ONE

# *Unwinding the twisted logic*
# *of competition*

# Competition by any other name

Myth #1: Free markets are competitive

It seems that at each stage of industrial progress a new monopoly has appeared to take hold of that era's critical technologies – be it railroads, oil, the internet or big data. Seven of the eight most valuable companies in the world today are tech companies: Apple (worth $961 billion), Microsoft ($946 billion), Amazon ($916 billion), Alphabet (the holding company for Google, worth $863 billion), Facebook ($512 billion), Alibaba (the 'Chinese Amazon', $480 billion) and Tencent (the 'Chinese Facebook', $472 billion).[1] For a sense of scale, oil company ExxonMobil is worth 'only' $343 billion. Facebook and Google together control 84 per cent of online advertising,[2] with advertising accounting for 97 per cent and 88 per cent of their total revenues respectively.[3] And if we were still in any doubt as to the economic might of these companies, Mark Zuckerberg reportedly used to end Facebook staff meetings by shouting: 'Domination!'[4]

When it comes to Big Tech, the list of transgressions is frightful: the proliferation of harmful and hateful content online; the spread of fake news and research; the commercialization of our personal information; violations of privacy; the exclusion of competitors from their platforms; the subversion of democracy; tax avoidance; poor treatment of workers; the creation of addictive products; the programmed prejudices of AI; the rising supremacy of robots over humans. These companies got to their positions of power through free market competition, having to prove that they had the best, most appealing products. But what about now? What keeps them at the top?

To a lay observer it is perplexing that these market-ruling companies are not besieged by the antitrust authorities – and indeed these companies probably feel that they are. But their deals consistently get the regulatory green light – from Facebook snapping up WhatsApp to Microsoft taking over Skype – and when their dominance is acknowledged and abuses are identified, the fines are footnotes to the balance sheet, even when they run up into the billions, and they generally come too late to make a difference to the market. The damage, by the end of whichever authority's lengthy investigation, has already been done.

Regulators have had trouble seeing past the prices – which are low or free – and the innovation and huge value brought to customers. But the costs are still there, they are just hidden upstream, in the prices paid by advertisers and passed on to customers in separate markets, or in the shadow prices paid by consumers in the form of their data, their time and their privacy. If the lay observer could see the problems, why couldn't the competition experts?

## *What is in a word?*

The first myth of the free market centres on a word: competition. The word 'competition' conjures up a world of fairness and excellence: where the playing field is level, the odds are even, and the winner deserves their prize. In markets, we are told, for there to be true competition, the players must be left to their own devices, free from oppressive and distorting regulation, free to compete and to be the best.

Our model of competition is simple: the presence of rivalry forces each of us to up our game. If everyone does this – strives to be the best that they can be – then collectively we will be the best that *we* can be, as a society. A competitive economy, it is assumed, will produce the greatest possible output at the least possible cost, and there will be no way to improve on the resulting allocation of resources, as long as the competition was fair and free.

Consumers, in particular, are singled out as beneficiaries of competition. In a competitive market, consumers get 'consumer welfare', in a very limited economic sense, by paying less for something than they were willing to. It is the boost you get when you go for an ice cream on a hot day, ready to part with £2 for a cone, only to find out that there are two rival ice cream stands and they are both charging just £1.50. That is £0.50 of consumer surplus hitting your utility-o-meter. You are welcome.

Consumer welfare goes up and down in reverse proportion to price – hence the theoretical focus of competition law on maintaining low prices for the benefit of consumers. If a company is able to obtain market power then it can raise its price above the competitive level – shifting that welfare from the consumer to its own pocket in the form of extra profits. And increasing the price also means that fewer people will buy the product, reducing output. Market power therefore benefits the company able to wield it, at the expense of the wider economy.

Unfortunately, perfect competition does not exist in reality. When there are quirks in the market that allow sellers to gain power over buyers, then it is as if these vendors have gained extra profits by exploiting a loophole (what economists would call a 'market failure'). Other market failures cause loopholes too: if a company has more information than customers then it can get away with charging more, or charging different amounts to different groups of people.

Another category of market failure is 'negative externalities' or 'spillovers'. These are costs that the company is able to externalize and on which the market does not put a price – I cannot charge drivers for polluting the air near my children's school, for example. So if there is no tax or law that otherwise discourages or prevents them, these spillovers present a profitable loophole for companies to exploit because they can make society pay for what would otherwise be a cost to their bottom line. The power to inflict these harms is downplayed by our models of competition. But these harms to society and the environment, which are not priced by the market system, accrue within the economic system anyway, acting as a lead weight dragging society and the economy down.

Competition is not just an economic principle, it is a cultural principle too, and we internalize it from an early age. It is what we teach our kids. An old episode from 1961 of the cartoon classic Looney Tunes, called *Daffy's Inn Trouble*, exemplifies the myth of competition. Daffy Duck is working as a cleaner at Porky Pig's saloon on the western frontier. Daffy is annoyed when Porky tells him he has a present to give him and it is nothing more than a new broom. Daffy quits in disgust and opens a rival tavern across the road. Competition ensues. Daffy offers free food and TV to customers to lure them away from Porky. Porky puts on a vaudeville show with live can-can girls, which prompts Daffy to try to put on his own cabaret show himself, in drag. Already customers have benefited – competition has spurred the expansion of services.

Daffy is frustrated by his inability to attract business, so he thinks, 'If you cannot beat them, why not join them?' He offers to go into partnership with Porky, first extending a friendly business proposition and then, when that does not work, threatening Porky with a pistol.

Then Daffy thinks again, 'If you cannot join them, why not destroy them?' He attempts to commit an act of corporate terrorism, entering Porky's restaurant in disguise, planting a bomb and then detonating it to flatten Porky's establishment. Unfortunately for Daffy, the explosion reveals a gushing oil well sitting under Porky's building. Porky develops the oil field and, now very well funded, puts a swanky hotel right next door, monopolizing the market. He rehires Daffy as a janitor, and the message is clear: cheating will not pay off, only those who deserve to win will be victorious.

What the episode also demonstrates, though, is that not all competition is good for consumers. If Porky had colluded with Daffy, or if Daffy's scheme to blow up Porky's inn had been successful, consumers, and indeed society, would have lost out. It was only luck and Porky's good character that preserved the benefits of competition, but it was ruthless competition that drove Daffy to his scheming. Daffy could just as easily have gotten away with it.

Competition that produces spillovers – allowing companies to pollute, to destabilize democracy, to endanger our health and to accumulate power for themselves – is not the good kind of competition we want to encourage. When we praise competition, there are various avenues we do not explore. How are the low prices for consumers achieved, and what else gets squeezed to lower them? If shareholders must be assured a return in competitive industries, who or what must accept less? Once the winner has won the race to dominance – then what? Different companies may have different levels of ability or willingness or cunning to inflict harm, but the competitor who finds a way to leverage externalities to earn additional profits can use this as a path to growth and therefore market power. Negative spillovers and market power, and the competition that births them both, are intimately connected.

This is a critical oversight lying unexamined in our economic theory of capitalism, shielded from view by the thicket of free market myths we will gradually untangle in this book. Beyond the impact of market power on prices, we have ignored most of the sources and kinds of power that matter. In particular, we have overlooked the power to impose negative spillovers on an unsuspecting society.

Economists acknowledge that spillovers exist. But the scale of them is vastly underappreciated, and they are treated as an afterthought. One UN-backed report in 2013 estimated that the global cost to the world economy of negative spillovers from sectors such as agriculture, forestry, fisheries, mining, oil and gas exploration and utilities is around $7.3 trillion a year (or around 10 per cent of global GDP) in damage to the environment, health and other vital systems on which humankind relies.[5] That is not a side issue, it is fast becoming the main issue of our times.

## *Are you concentrating?*

What does it mean to call markets 'free'? On the one hand it could just mean that they are unregulated – free from government intervention. But we usually also take it to mean that they are competitive – that no one party controls them, that many companies hawk and trade in a diverse and bustling market. And yet, all around us, rivals are merging, or failing, with industries playing host to fewer and fewer competitors. The evidence shows that competition is giving way to monopoly across the economy.

Concentration is everywhere. Three firms, American Express, MasterCard and Visa, control over 90 per cent of the US credit card market, and four firms account for two-thirds of the UK market.[6] Three companies control 70 per cent of the world's pesticide market, 80 per cent of the US corn-seed market, and overall just six companies control the entirety of global agribusiness.[7] Ninety per cent of the planted acreage of cotton in the US uses the seeds of one company – Monsanto (recently merged with rival Bayer).[8] Two companies – Boeing and Airbus – have a worldwide duopoly in civil aviation. Two corporations control 90 per cent of the beer that Americans drink, and one of those companies, Anheuser-Busch InBev, sells one in five beers drunk on the planet.[9] Five banks control about half of the banking assets in America.[10] In the UK, the 100 biggest firms now account for nearly a quarter of total revenue, up 25 per cent since 2004.[11] Of the ten most important consumer markets in the UK, accounting for 40 per cent of consumer spending, eight are classed as 'concentrated', including groceries, broadband, mobile telephony, landline-only phone contracts, electricity, gas, personal current accounts, and credit cards.[12] And on and on.

This is not an isolated phenomenon, restricted to a few discrete markets. One study finds that 75 per cent of industries in the US have experienced a reduction in the number of competitors and a corresponding increase in levels of industry concentration in the last two decades.[13] There is a similar trend across Europe, with 80 per cent of industries showing an increase in concentration.[14]

And the evidence is finally emerging that concentration leads to exactly the consequences we feared it might. Despite competition authorities blessing almost all industry tie-ups, a 2016 study by the US Federal Reserve showed that most mergers actually lead to price mark-ups, with little evidence of greater efficiency.[15] A retrospective review of dozens of mergers found that post-merger prices rose in the vast majority of cases.[16] The free market competition served up by competition enforcers is not even delivering low prices, let alone the other supposed benefits of competition.

Perhaps unsurprisingly, then, corporate profits are at an all-time high, coming at the expense of both wages and corporate investment.[17] Studies indicate that these increased profits have come off the back of price increases, indicative of market power. Firms now charge a mark-up of 61 per cent over cost, as compared to 21 per cent in 1980. Mark-ups have risen not just in America but in Europe as well.[18] As we might expect, profits have increased the most in the industries where competition has floundered, and wage growth has been the most anaemic in those same industries.[19]

Taken together, these economic indicators tell a strong story of the accretion and exercise of market power across the economy. The whole system is becoming more concentrated, changing the fundamental balance of power between the corporate sector, the state and society. Free market competition seems to really mean freedom for monopolists.

The companies occupying the remaining slots in these depopulated markets do well for themselves, but the economy suffers. High concentration leads to lower productivity, lower wages for workers, and higher prices. It also inhibits business dynamism, meaning fewer brave souls take the leap to start up a business in the first place.

We have stopped being able to perceive this rise in corporate power, even though it is all around us. Until very recently hardly anyone seemed to notice the growing trend of concentration, despite the recognition that our economies are languishing. It is an economic reality to which we have slowly become acclimatized: a hyper-concentrated industrial landscape dominated by big companies, and a free rein to capital deployed through corporations. It is as if the whole world is struggling to breathe but we have failed to realize that companies are taking up all the oxygen. In fact, this is more than metaphoric. Companies fell forests, depleting our life-giving resources, whilst exhaling greenhouse gases and other pollutants through their production processes, which we breathe in and which our atmosphere absorbs like second-hand smoke.

Free markets are supposed to bring us growth and technological advancement, so if we could believe the myth that our
markets were competitive then the costs might be worth it. But
actually the very opposite is true: free markets seem to inevitably turn into concentrated ones, ostensibly with the regulatory
blessing of antitrust authorities. And with that market concentration comes unaccountable power. So, Walmart, the world's
biggest retailer, can use its prodigious scale to deliver cheap
groceries but it can also make or break an entire local economy. BP can siphon and supply oil from and to any point on
the Earth's surface, but it can also obliterate an ecosystem
when it loses control of one of its wells. The bigger companies
get, the greater the potential rewards but also the bigger the
public exposure to their mistakes and misdeeds. If big companies can do no wrong – and there is, in any case, no one to hold
them accountable if they do – who is to guard the grain stores
of public value from being ransacked?

## Rich man, poor man, beggar man, thief

The rise in corporate power is not self-contained in the corporate world, it spills over into personal wealth. Far from the myth
of competitive markets dispersing power, we have a capitalist
system that concentrates power in the name of competition.

Just as corporate power is growing, so too are the wealth
and power of the richest 1 per cent. The numbers beggar belief.
Since 1980, the top 1 per cent captured 27 per cent of new
income globally, whilst the bottom 50 per cent laid claim to
only 12 per cent.[20] In 2018, just twenty-six people owned the
same amount of wealth as the 3.8 billion people who make up
the poorest half of humanity, down from forty-three people the
year before.[21] The funnelling of corporate profits towards
shareholders makes this trend worse. The proportion of GDP

that is extracted by shareholders amounts to a transfer of $2 trillion of annual income going to investors, at the expense of consumers, workers and the planet.[22]

It turns out that the richest people get a substantial portion of their wealth through shareholdings in companies. America's top 0.1 per cent of wealthy households hold around a third of their wealth in equities.[23] And 77 per cent of capital income – dividends, interest and capital gains – is concentrated in the top 10 per cent of people.[24] The middle classes invest most of their wealth in their homes, and this wealth tends to be offset or overwhelmed by mortgage debt. The rich hold only around 8 per cent of their wealth through land or property whilst investing 26 per cent of their savings in stocks.[25] The wealthy derive a significant proportion of their wealth from companies designed and set up to serve the interests of shareholders and, as we shall see, these companies are predominantly owned by the wealthy.

Shareholder value therefore promotes the interests of the wealthiest 10 per cent, at the expense of the rest. The picture looks even starker if you zoom out and follow the money, as it flows to elite shareholders off the back of the gruelling work carried out by impoverished people located elsewhere in the world. Although many workers around the world do own shares, shareholder value bears down in the harshest terms on vast swathes of society – and workers' holdings are not great enough to compensate, nor could they ever really be.

We also know that market power wielded against consumers in product markets makes distributional issues worse. The price of essential goods includes an uplift to the monopolist and a kickback to the shareholder, with a ripple effect all the way down the affordability ladder. Market power hits poorer people hardest, with monopoly rents transferred to shareholders, who tend already to be rich.[26] One estimate finds that for each dollar of monopoly profits, a total of $0.37 is transferred from the 90 per cent poorest to the 10 per cent richest.[27] The mass of people are harmed by monopoly, and only a few benefit.

The possible causes of inequality are, of course, multiple and complex: globalization and automation driving down workers' wages, technology delivering unprecedented wealth to a few elite individuals, lower levels of union activity reducing workers' bargaining power. But the principle that companies should maximize profits for shareholders only, known as 'shareholder value', and the reality of growing market power, have also played their part.

Money transferred to shareholders is not recirculated into the economy: much of it disappears out of the system. It is estimated that $7.6 trillion of wealth is legally hidden in tax havens across the world.[28] The economy is run for shareholders but they are not reinvesting in the real economy, they are extracting value from the stock market. This leaves a vacuum that companies must continually fill – with cost savings from lowering the cost of production or job cuts, or cost-shifting externalities, or price increases achieved through market power.[29]

We can look at the ten richest people in the world, according to the 2018 Forbes rich list, and find that each one of them derived their wealth from corporate activities. The richest two people in the world, Jeff Bezos and Bill Gates, own companies that need no introduction; number 3 is Warren Buffett whose Berkshire Hathaway invests in and owns many other companies; number 4 is Bernard Arnault, who owns luxury brands like Louis Vuitton; Carlos Slim is number 5 and a major investor in Mexican telecoms; Amancio Ortega is the sixth richest person and the world's richest retailer, with interests in brands like Zara, one of the companies whose clothes were produced at Rana Plaza; Larry Ellison, who co-founded the software firm Oracle in the 1970s, is number 7; number 8 is Mark Zuckerberg; number 9 is Michael Bloomberg; and number 10 is Larry Page, the co-founder of Google. Shareholder value and free market competition has certainly worked well for them and for the other 2,153 billionaires on the list, who between them were worth a total of $8.7 trillion, much of that wealth coming from corporate interests. What we see is that wealth does not only come from inheritance, land ownership, hard work and good luck: corporations are designed to solidify wealth and power, and the rich have taken advantage of that. And the rising inequality that results should really be no surprise when 157 of the top 200 economic entities in the world are corporations, not countries.[30]

With markets growing ever more concentrated, and companies owned by the wealthy few, the idea that free market competition results in prosperity and freedom for the many begins to take on an absurd aspect. In fact, the vast majority of the value of publicly listed companies comes from their market power.[31] Market dominance signals a good investment, as does the ability to create unregulated spillovers. And it makes sense: if a company has no power, either to increase its prices or reduce its costs, then it will have no excess rents to distribute, in which case why would anyone invest when there are other companies with market power offering higher returns? Looking at the FTSE 100 we should not therefore be shocked to see that British American Tobacco is still amongst the top 10 companies, ranked by market capitalization. Royal Dutch Shell is number 1.

## Power to the powerful

The seemingly unavoidable tendency within capitalism is for power and money to accumulate, and the freer the market – with less government intervention and less market-distorting taxation – the more this will be so. Money breeds money, and we do not redistribute it nearly enough to compensate for that, because we are worried about dampening the incentive to make more money. We buy into the contrary myth that markets are competitive: money will spread out through the economy, we think, to those who compete and win.

Modern economics has catalogued the ways in which companies are able to build up competitive moats to defend their monopolistic positions – from exploiting first mover advantages, network effects and customer switching costs, to using information asymmetries, contractual bargaining power and intellectual property rights to entrench their dominance. Recent Nobel prizes have been won for these very observations.* It is clear that, left to themselves, markets veer almost inevitably towards concentration. The mechanisms by which this is achieved are myriad, and companies – chasing a return and a reprieve from competition – are designed to seek them out.

Recent research by economist Thomas Piketty and his colleagues has also shown that there is indeed a natural propensity for capital to accumulate.[32] Capital income from investments, such as from interest and dividends, will end up less evenly distributed than labour income from work. The exception is executive pay. The executives and managers that head up large firms and banks, technically still 'workers', have become untethered from the rest of society, floating in a separate, rarefied ether made of money. They are able to exercise bargaining power in company hierarchies by sitting on each other's remuneration committees, awarding each other bonuses, share options and pay increases, and thereby earning 'super salaries' that are completely unrelated to their actual productivity, performance or market forces. Either way, through capital investments or their pay, the rich get richer.

*Nobel prizes on this topic were awarded to Joseph Stiglitz, Michael Spence and George Akerlof in 2001; Peter Diamond, Christopher Pissarides and Dale Mortensen in 2010; and Jean Tirole in 2014.

The general response is that we do not need to worry about escalating wealth because economic dynamism will keep inequality at bay. Even if the rich get richer, the poor will get richer too. But in fact, as Piketty shows, the only times when inequality has actually declined in the last two hundred years are when capital itself has been destroyed (through two world wars) or when income has been aggressively redistributed via progressive taxation at rates considered unthinkable today – with top income tax rates of over 90 per cent in the UK and US around the Second World War. Capitalism itself is not an equalizer.

## Competition? It's a matter of perspective

The impulse of competition to create wealth and power is perhaps most clear in relation to tech markets. How have the tech giants emerged from a decade of phenomenal growth and market domination more or less unscathed by antitrust inquiry? How could the antitrust community convince itself that Google, with a 90 per cent market share in search, still faces significant competition? To fight their way out of this intellectual corner, competition lawyers and economists have historically relied upon the concept of 'contestability'. In the internet age, they insist, competition is just 'one click away' – even Google supposedly exists in a highly contested market, replete with potential competitors. Monopoly would have no chance to endure: there are no barriers to entry, as anyone can start a website, and the constant churn of start-ups is evidence of vigorous competition.

If you can still call this competition, though, it is a version that seems to primarily benefit the few not the many. In fact, it appears to be a bit of a sham. Contestability conjures the image of Gulliver besieged by the Lilliputians, or the Earth's atmosphere battered by cosmic rays. It relies on the idea that even big companies face relentless competition from the small guys trying to chip away at their market power and from potential competitors waiting in the wings. But the reality is closer to the nineteenth-century Wimbledon tennis tournaments where the defending champion did not have to play any of the heats and therefore faced their weary challenger in the final fresh and energized. Unsurprisingly, a few winners dominated the championships year after year.

Contestability assumes that even very large firms in concentrated markets would be forced to behave competitively and price as if they are, in fact, facing competition, even if they are not. It neatly encapsulates the unshakeable faith in free markets and the myth that free markets are competitive even when they do not seem to be. This 'as if' was articulated by economist Milton Friedman, a doyen of the neoliberal Chicago School of economics, expressing his admiration for the monopolistic economy: 'I have become increasingly impressed,' he said, 'with how wide is the range of problems and industries for which it is appropriate to treat the economy *as if* it were competitive'.[33] As if, Friedman, as if.

This hypothetical competition has proven to be illusory in practice too. High profits are not enticing start-ups into industry, in part because the incumbents use their excess profits to create a walled garden: they lobby for precisely the kind of regulation that would keep smaller entrants out.[34] It turns out that monopolists can and have lasted decades, and that it is very wishful thinking to assume that a usurper is just around the corner and that we can continue to allow the incumbent to bed down in the meantime. There is little empirical evidence of potential entry restraining monopolists' activities, even in those markets where entry is supposed to be more likely.[35] Let's take the supposed low barriers to entry of digital markets – yes, anyone with a computer, a server and access to the internet is free to clone the entire Facebook site, including all its features (if we were to ignore intellectual property laws). But that does not mean they could convince a single user to use the new service, because the value in Facebook comes from the users, and specifically from the 'network effects' – the value for each individual user of the network of other users already using the service.

Could Facebook really be 'blindsided by a start-up in a garage or an unexpected technological shift' as *The Economist* once suggested?[36] Not if, along with the other tech giants, it continues to police the 'kill zone', hoovering up or squashing any potential competitors, ensuring that venture capitalists will not invest in technologies into which they know these companies are moving, effectively eliminating the possibility of potential competition. As it stands, Google, Apple, Microsoft, Facebook and Amazon occupy pole positions across a number of technologies, including search, mail, messaging, maps, cloud computing, social networking, AI, autonomous vehicles and digital advertising.

It remains unclear that rivalry between just a few enormous firms replicates the consumer benefits of classic competition between many small players.[37]

And so the word competition has become a code word for domination, on the assumption that as long as prices are low – which they are assumed already to be – then the accumulation of power does not matter. It would be a truly wondrous system, if it were real.

## A word of caution

The mythology of free markets begins with the word 'competition'. Competition means the rivalry of many small companies, or it means the defence of a dominant market position by a monopolist. Competition means the race to the top, or it can mean the never-ending victory lap. Competition means competing fairly, but there is much foul play that the rules of the game ignore. As antitrust reformer Matt Stoller explains, alongside our submission to free markets, we have somehow lost the words to describe and identify corporate power: 'Words like "liberty" and "markets" and "competition" and "monopoly" and "citizen",' he says, 'have been perverted, taken by technocrats who hide the levers of power from most of us.'[38] We call a market competitive when it is actually monopolistic and rife with externalities and inefficiencies: it is free only in the sense that it is a free-for-all.

Our idea of competition is tied up with morality, in particular the notion that in a free market people get what they deserve, like industrious Porky versus dastardly Daffy. But success on the market has as much to do with luck as it does with skill (like the oil well discovered under Porky's inn), and any company experiencing commercial success does so by standing on the shoulders of many giants – from its workers, its customers and the state, to prior innovations, public resources, public infrastructure and the natural environment. But instead of fulfilling their debts to society, we see corporations shifting their profits offshore to hide them from tax liability – to the tune of trillions in undeclared revenues.

Politicians of all stripes can agree that we should have more competition, whilst harbouring very different visions of how markets should work. We applaud competition, but free markets do not create a multiplicity of options and dispersed power. Instead, markets inevitably tend to consolidate, and yet we often still label the results 'competitive'. If this is the case then it is likely that we are vastly under-reacting to corporate power, naively assuming that it soon shall pass. Rather, we must look at ramping up antitrust enforcement and challenging power itself. Business success should come with greater responsibility, not just to share the wealth through the redistributive system of taxation but also to share the accompanying power.

The objection will be that this is unfair – why should we target successful companies? Won't this hinder their performance? If we punish big companies for being successful by saddling them with more responsibility then will it not kill the market dynamism of capitalism, which brings us innovation, well-being and, well, stuff? But the truth is that monopolies and powerful companies, earning above-competitive prices by taking advantage of some market failure, can afford to do some good. And if it turns out that taking care of their broader stakeholders so hobbles a powerful company, or sends it into bankruptcy, then we should question the legitimacy of their original business model: it was likely built on the co-opting of public value and little more.

We cannot get away from the word 'competition', we are stuck with it. But when we come across it we can be on our guard, recognizing that people often use it in paradoxical ways, as a cover for what is really better described as the process of attempting to accumulate power – whether legitimately or illegitimately, whether successfully or not. Currently, many markets are highly concentrated, as the evidence shows. If someone claims a market is competitive, they must mean something other than free from market power – and certainly they cannot mean it is free from spillovers, as almost no market is. Think twice whenever you come across the word. What does it really mean? You have been warned.

---

**SUMMARY**

**Myth #1:** Free markets are competitive.

**Reality:** Free market competition creates power. In fact, 'competition' has come to be synonymous with domination and corporate power.

---

## 2.

# *This is your brain on shareholder value*

Myth #2: Companies compete by trying to best respond
to the needs of society

In March 2019, almost exactly six years after Rana Plaza, I found myself in a room full of rebels planning peaceful acts of civil disobedience. The objective of the meeting was to force political action on climate change.[1] This was not a ragtag pack of rabble-rousers, these were my peers: philanthropists, scientists, lawyers, politicians, students, and one sixteen-year-old girl, busy with exams and teenage life, who told us about how one day she was so overcome with grief for the fate of her generation that she sat down in the street and wept.

The degradation of the planet is proceeding at a devastating pace, with the impact of human activities driving each one of the planet's vital ecological systems, from the climate to the freshwater cycle, to the brink of catastrophic failure. It could be five, ten or twenty years until we face social and environmental collapse, depending on your levels of optimism.[2] By some estimates, the temperature of the planet is set to rise by almost 5°C by the end of the century, bringing with it floods, droughts, storms and a rise in sea levels that will jeopardize all life on Earth.[3] We have over-exploited the agricultural land, the water and the fisheries, as well as using them as dumping grounds for waste and plastic. The list goes on.

Accepting the reality of climate change invites cognitive dissonance: companies compete by trying to best serve our needs, driving forward innovation and allocating resources in the economy in just the best possible way – how can this have led to ruin? The existential threat faced by our species, after decades of careless disregard for the natural systems on which we depend, is as stark an example as can be found of our supposedly rational, just, innovative and generous economic system being anything but. An efficient and desirable system does not destroy itself with its own emissions, and it would not harm the most vulnerable and marginalized first.

We have had plenty of warning that the profit-is-everything way of doing business might be our undoing. On the night of 20 April 2010, in the Gulf of Mexico, there was an almighty explosion at the Deepwater Horizon oil rig, operated on behalf of oil giant BP.[4] Highly combustible gas flooded the rig, coating the crew from head to toe as they ran for cover from shrapnel and debris. Those who could, piled into the lifeboats as the smoke and heat began to overwhelm the workers stuck on the rig's deck. Some jumped the sixty feet into the water and swam for their lives. The rig began to leak what would end up being 4.9 million barrels of petroleum into the ocean. This was the largest marine oil spill in history, which would take eighty-seven days to get under control. The disaster killed eleven people, hundreds of dolphins, over 100,000 birds and billions of fish. The environmental damage was catastrophic.

The cause? Running weeks behind schedule and tens of millions of dollars over budget, BP and its contractors implemented dangerous cost-cutting measures in the construction of the well. Eager to close up what was known as 'the well from hell', as the project neared its end, the crew were encouraged to drill fast and get out of there. Meanwhile, despite daily safety briefings, the crew had not been trained for the worst.

The Deepwater Horizon oil spill is a poignant example of one way in which the free market logic can come unstuck, when a steely-eyed focus on profits and nothing else causes a company to make decisions that clearly do not serve the public good, and in fact are not even in the company's own best interests. BP had to pay out $65 billion in compensation. The planet picked up the rest of the bill.

## The shareholder value company

The myth of efficient and competitive free markets relies on another myth: the myth of the efficient company. The economics of free market competition assume that firms will seek to maximize profits, and that this is what drives efficiency. Capital will never rest, it will constantly search for a better investment, a better return, and, in the meantime, consumers benefit from cheap goods whilst their every priceable need is met. Owners of capital will receive some profit, enough to make a living, to compensate them for putting their money to work instead of spending it on themselves. Since companies are so miraculously efficient, and creative, and innovative, and since this means we will get the most economic output and the best allocation of resources we could hope for as a society through corporate self-interest, this myth leaves us so very grateful to the investors that make this sacrifice to finance our corporations and therefore our society.

But companies can choose how they make their profits – how to pursue power and returns for shareholders – within what the law will allow, and the law currently allows the expulsion of many costs from the corporate balance sheet over to the societal balance sheet, all under the principle of 'shareholder value'. Antitrust does not consider this unfair competition and does not recognize this sort of power.

The protection of shareholder interests, in and of itself, is a sensible idea. Shareholders invest their money, they do not always get to control how it is managed, and the law of corporate governance is partly there to make sure that unwitting investors are not taken advantage of by lazy or wasteful executives. Shareholders accept the risk that they may receive no return for their investment, may even lose their original contribution, but they do so on the back of the enticing promise that they have some claim over the company's gains, and it therefore makes sense that they would want the managers of the company to work towards securing those gains. But taken to the extreme, as it has been by modern economists, legal scholars and business people themselves, 'shareholder value' creates a duty not just to consider shareholder interests but to prioritize them above all others, to equate shareholder 'interests' with financial returns only, and not just to deliver such returns but to ensure their *maximization*.

Shareholder value took hold as a business strategy in the 1970s. How did companies lose all sense of responsibility other than to shareholders? How did the principle of shareholder value become entrenched? And why do we continue to assume that this lack of responsibility will somehow serve the public interest?

## Milton Freedom

The most famous, or indeed infamous, defender of shareholder value was Milton Friedman. Friedman and I have two things in common: we are connected via my husband's grandfather, who was one of his PhD students at Chicago, and we are both five foot two. He was known to be loud and argumentative (okay, maybe that's three things we have in common) and he was obsessed with free markets – he even made a TV show about it.

Neoliberal thinking on corporate governance took shape in the context of the post-war economy in which the future of the free market stood imperilled. This spurred Milton Friedman, Friedrich Hayek and other disgruntled economists to form a free marketeers club – the Mont Pelerin Society – founded to save market liberalism. Their campaign to rehabilitate free market capitalism, and to protect the freedom of capital from state control, was astonishingly successful, and Friedman himself, through his single-minded and relentless focus, had a huge impact on economic policy and the business world. Most importantly for our inquiry, he lent intellectual rigour to the concept of shareholder value.

One of his most influential pieces of work was, in fact, not a peer-reviewed journal article or his Nobel-winning research. It was an op-ed piece in the *New York Times Magazine*, published in 1970. Titled 'The Social Responsibility of Business is to Increase its Profits', it is often cited as the seminal pronouncement on shareholder value.

Shocking readers at the time, Friedman argued that it is the only proper goal of business, and indeed its social responsibility, to maximize profits for the benefit of shareholders.[5] Managers should not get distracted by trying to use private money for public good. In fact, this would imperil the efficiency of the company. Instead, companies should be run on behalf of their shareholders only. In a free market, so the mantra goes, the rest will take care of itself.

What Friedman was fighting against at the time was what he, and others in the Chicago School, perceived to be the 'already too prevalent view' that the 'pursuit of profits is wicked and immoral and must be curbed and controlled'.[6] The profit motive is so universal now that it can be hard to remember a time when it was thought of as abhorrent, but when Friedman started waging his campaign, just after the Great Depression, unregulated capitalism lay manifestly discredited.

According to Friedman, though, shareholders should be free to make money through corporations, and express themselves as consumers and investors through the markets. The highest possible good would flow from this self-interest. The opposite view – that business should take on broader responsibilities – was, for Friedman, one step removed from communism. It was as bad, possibly worse, than government itself intervening in markets. Writing in the midst of the Cold War, he argued that businessmen who say that business should not 'merely' be focused on profit, but should be concerned with providing employment, eliminating discrimination, or avoiding pollution 'are – or would be if they or anyone else took them seriously – preaching pure and unadulterated socialism. Businessmen who talk this way are unwitting puppets of the intellectual forces that have been undermining the basis of a free society these past decades.'[7] In promoting shareholder value, neoliberal thinkers like Friedman felt themselves to be 'foot-soldiers in the fight against communism'.[8] Accommodating social responsibility within the corporation, he thought, would push free market America ever closer towards Soviet collectivism and totalitarianism.

## How do shareholder value companies compete?

There was a time when doing business did not necessarily mean operating a company. Before corporations, if you wanted to join assets or resources with someone else, you had to come up with a complex contract to set out all the terms and distribute all the financial risks, and you had to do that every time. Economist Ronald Coase took this inefficient system as a basis for why the business firm must exist. Coase's insight was that forming a company would have a distinct advantage over repeated, ad hoc interactions between individuals operating in the market: it would limit the 'transaction costs' of entering into new contracts every time you wanted to get something done.[9] What had to be done through contracting on the market could be smoothly achieved with a kind of command and control in the hierarchy of a company.

In the 1930s, Coase, then a young socialist, visited Detroit and pondered how people could be so opposed to communist economic planning when the Ford Motor Company, a large and vertically integrated firm, was in essence a privately owned, planned bureaucracy, not unlike the Soviet Union. For Coase, the difference between the two was efficiency: the firm would limit its scale, the boundaries of its domain and its extent of integration with competitors and suppliers, to that which was most efficient. The communist state could not be relied upon to do the same.

This view came to be highly influential in the Chicago School approach towards companies, and big companies in particular. But what Coase's theory failed to acknowledge was that there may be a difference between efficiency-enhancing profit maximization on the one hand and spillover-inducing shareholder wealth maximization on the other, which can transform a company from a vessel for consumer welfare into a vehicle for power and externalities. Indeed, the firm's boundaries are determined by what the market and the law will allow, not by efficiency. If pushing those boundaries allows for a greater financial return for investors, the shareholder value company will happily encroach on the public sphere to satisfy the need for profits. Efficiency poses no restraint when the costs are not fully counted.

Viewing shareholder value as a mechanism for value extraction casts corporate activities in a different light. Gone is the myth of earnest companies competing to meet our needs. Instead, if bewitched by the spell of shareholder value, companies will do whatever it takes to get to our wallets, hoovering up cash for the benefit of shareholders only. It is what the shareholder value imperative demands; it is what companies have been designed to do.

Even though economic theory touts consumer welfare as the windfall of competitive markets, companies are busy trying to limit consumer welfare and channel it into producer profits wherever possible. This is the essence of much management training and business education: lessons in how to evade competitive pressure. According to Michael Porter's 'Five Forces' model, for example, the least attractive industry for investment and enterprise will be one in which profitability is systematically eroded by the Five Forces of competition:

- industry rivalry
- the threat of substitute products
- the bargaining power of suppliers
- the bargaining power of buyers, and
- the threat of new entrants.

Antitrust law, in theory, tries to dial up the intensity of each of these forces, or prevent any barriers from arising that would mitigate their effects. But, of course, avoiding competition is precisely what the business executive is trying to achieve.

For example, instead of competing with their rivals, which destroys corporate value, companies can attempt to collude. As a junior lawyer, when I was tasked with poring over thousands of emails amassed as potential evidence of a collusive conspiracy, I was generally struck by the observation that they were not the obviously conniving communications of evil conspirators. The emails told funny, sad and ultimately human stories of health problems, divorce, children's birthdays and weddings. They also documented the intense pressure piled on to mid-level managers in rival companies to deliver financial results. It seemed that it was precisely the pressure of competition that drove those managers to fix prices or to agree to stay out of each other's sales territory.

One of the most famous cartel cases of recent decades was what the FBI dubbed the case of the 'Harvest King'. The FBI became involved because the conspiracy to increase prices in the market for a product called lysine – a growth-enhancing additive fed to animals to fatten them up for human consumption – was uncovered with the help of an informant. Mark Whitacre, played by Matt Damon in the Hollywood adaptation of this remarkable story, *The Informant!*, was a PhD biochemist working for Archer Daniels Midland, an agrochemical company operating out of the fertile lands of Decatur, Illinois. Whitacre, a rising star in the company, was embezzling money from ADM – he would eventually steal at least $9 million by submitting phony invoices for work done by contractors, and funnelling the proceeds into offshore and Swiss bank accounts. He unwittingly involved the FBI in his attempt to cover his own tracks when he accused a competitor of industrial sabotage. He realized that the FBI would soon figure out what he had been up to so he confessed and agreed to help the authorities crack down on the global lysine cartel.

The court documents revealed the spirit of the conspiracy. ADM President James Randall had baldly proclaimed that: 'Our competitors are our friends. Our customers are the enemy.' Such pronouncements were not unusual in the 1990s, but this statement belies the true lengths to which a company will go to secure a profit. The lysine competitors spied on each other, fabricated aliases, lied, cheated, extorted, obstructed justice, and hired prostitutes to gather information from competitors (that is how they treated their 'friends'!). They also formed a fake trade association as a cover for their cartel meetings. In one such meeting, secretly filmed by Whitacre, the participants joked about the FBI and antitrust authorities finding out about what they were doing. They knew full well it was illegal, but the risk was well worth it.

ADM is a public company, listed on the New York Stock Exchange, and at the time it had $14 billion in global sales and

23,000 employees. At trial, the US Court of Appeals for the Seventh Circuit described 'an inexplicable lack of business ethics and an atmosphere of general lawlessness that infected the very heart of one of America's leading corporate citizens'.[10] But, in fact, it is not inexplicable. It can be easily explained by the relentless driver of shareholder value and the search for market power, however it may be achieved. Efficient? Companies are certainly efficient at generating schemes to make money – it is another question whether the public at large benefits.

If a company cannot join with a competitor, though – through collusion or merger – then it can seek to destroy them. What happens when you start carrying shareholder value and market power around with you in your pocket? Facebook has a track record of using dubious methods to establish its market position. Confidential documents seized by the UK Parliament showed that Facebook was ruthless in cutting off access to its services for apps like Vine, a video-sharing app, created by Twitter and subsequently shut down. Facebook used an app called Onavo to monitor users without their knowledge, including to identify frequently used rival apps, which helped them to decide which apps to buy and which to try to shut down or clone.[11] The evidence showed that whilst the antitrust authorities were unable to identify the competitive threat that WhatsApp posed to Facebook, perfunctorily rubber-stamping the merger, the company itself knew precisely how much the rival app was being used and therefore the upside of eliminating that competition.

A single-minded focus on profits forces companies to pursue all available means of obtaining power and lowering costs. The DuPont case shows how generating social harm can be a perfectly rational business strategy – perhaps especially for big firms, for whom the potentially enormous litigation costs and fines are not critical.[12] C8 is a chemical that DuPont used in the making of Teflon in its West Virginia plant. At least since 1984, DuPont knew that C8 is toxic, does not break down in the environment, accumulates in human blood, travels from pregnant mothers to their babies, and seeps into local drinking water supplies. But, after a careful cost–benefit analysis, and ignoring the recommendations of their legal and medical departments, DuPont decided to continue with, and even scale up, C8 emissions.

Internal documents show that polluting was a rational decision for DuPont: under reasonable probabilities of detection, choosing to pollute was an optimal strategy from the company's perspective, even if the cost of preventing pollution was lower than the cost of the health damages produced. The debacle cost the company close to $1 billion, so you might ask how can that be good for shareholders? But the company was able to use its informational advantage over regulators to hide the true costs of C8 for decades, which meant that the company could earn profits in the meantime but the litigation and regulatory costs would not catch up with them until years later. And even then, payment of compensation could be delayed or paid in instalments.

Companies can also compete by cutting costs we would rather not have them cut. Amazon's low prices to consumers may be subsidized by high fees to merchants and may be motivated by a desire to dominate not just one market but all the markets. BP can cut costs in building a well but the result is the Deepwater Horizon disaster. In the case of the 1990s 'banana wars', UK supermarkets were able to cut the price of bananas because suppliers were willing to reduce costs. Fair trade groups documented that in 1999 Del Monte sacked all 4,300 of its workers on one of its biggest plantations in Costa Rica, and then rehired them on wages that were cut by half, with longer hours and fewer benefits.[13] Cost cutting puts pressure on production, including on the real human beings doing the work, who must tolerate longer working days or lower wages, and deliver higher productivity.

Competition is a race to monopoly as firms elbow each other out of the way to get to higher profits. And things can get ugly. As recently as 2004, a popular business book encouraged companies to pursue shareholder value to 'win' in the marketplace.[14] These firms should be 'willing to hurt their rivals', to be 'ruthless' and 'mean', and 'enjoy watching their competitors squirm'. They should do whatever it takes to win, going up to the very edge of illegality. And if they go over the line then the penalties, even if big, will be nothing in relation to the winnings. When audit firm Ernst & Young surveyed nearly 400 chief financial officers, it found that a worryingly high percentage, 13 per cent, would be willing to make cash payments to win or retain business.[15]

People point to the landmark antitrust case against Microsoft in the 1990s as releasing the computer market from Bill Gates' grip and paving the way for new technologies and platforms. They use it as a reason to break up Facebook and Google – *look, the world didn't crumble, in fact it thrived.* But clipping Microsoft's wings gave only a brief reprieve, because the new competitors were competing to be exactly like Microsoft had been, and Microsoft is still a substantial force in technology. Like the many-headed Hydra of Greek mythology, cutting down one power-hungry company spawns five others in its wake. Seeking market dominance is a reliable way to guarantee shareholder returns, and history shows us that creating more competition is only ever a temporary measure. AT&T made way for Microsoft; Microsoft made way for Google – the demolition of one monopoly merely readies the field for another to take its place or, more usually, to amble alongside it. Breaking up companies is not enough.

Companies competing to maximize profits will always be devising ways to do so at public expense – either by avoiding competition in order to increase prices, or by shifting costs on to society in the form of negative spillovers. Stronger enforcement against monopolies would help. But whilst making markets more competitive may lead to lower prices for consumers, we must ask how long it will last, and how are those low prices achieved? Without addressing the fundamental driver within the company to pursue profits at any cost, it is like trying to hold back the tide with our bare hands.

---

**SUMMARY**

**Myth #2:** Companies compete by trying to best respond to the needs of society.

**Reality:** Companies compete for power, for the benefit of their shareholders, in ways that harm society.

---

## 3.

## *In big we trust*

Myth #3: Corporate power is benign

Finance is a field of constant innovation, the poster child for the abundance of the free market. The financial system serves many essential roles in our economy and society – allowing us to save for big expenditures and old age, to borrow, to invest, to build up our economies and to bankroll expansion. But despite leaps in technology and computing, the financial system has not increased its productivity in the last 100 years – it is barely more efficient now than it was a century ago.[1] And the opportunism and exploitation baked into this system also expose another side to free markets: that those that most need protecting are most vulnerable to the injustices and vicissitudes of the market. Pay-day lending, subprime mortgages, Credit Default Swaps – each of these is innovative in its own way, but on closer inspection each one relies on persistent imbalance and inequality. They allow the rich to gamble and trade on the vulnerability and desperation of the poor.

It is often claimed that markets are neutral, and the only distortion of power we need be concerned with is market power – the ability of some firms to undermine competition and increase prices above competitive levels. Indeed, competition is thought to dissipate power (Myth #1), as any undeserved power will be competed away by rivals entering the market, and even big companies either face such potential competition or act as if they do. But the market is actually suffused with the power of shareholder value companies that operate not based on efficiency (Myth #2) but in the pursuit of power. That power does not disperse and does not incidentally serve the public interest – it supports an infrastructure that benefits the wealthy and the already powerful.

## An economy for the fittest

At least since the Industrial Revolution, we have been debating how to split the proceeds of the economic pie between those who fund it, those who bake it and those who eat it. The solution we have landed on in the Anglo-American capitalist system is brilliantly simple: we let the markets decide. We carve off narrow spaces for public provision – some but not all education, some but not all health care, some but not all national defence – but otherwise it is free markets all the way. Why? Because economic theory – at least the narrow version co-opted by economic policymakers – tells us that free market competition will generate the maximum 'efficiency' and everyone, including investors, workers and consumers, will be better off. If there are distributional issues, there is a neat solution: we can grow the size of the pie.*

The caveats that the economist would add – that this only works if property rights are fully allocated, if bargaining power is equal, if information is transparent – rarely, if ever, apply in practice. There is also much that this model ignores – idiosyncrasies of human institutions and human behaviour – and still more that the market cannot value and therefore treats as worthless. Nor is

* These ideas are based on a branch of economics called 'neoclassical' economics. See the Glossary at the back of the book for more.

it obvious that we actually can grow our way out of this mess, since we appear to have grown our way directly into it.

This focus on the markets also obscures the frequent dissonance between our actions as consumers and our political beliefs, and the reliable inconsistency of our economic decision making, which has been well evidenced by behavioural economists such as Daniel Kahneman. Mark Sagoff writes that:

> [L]ike members of the public generally, I, too, have divided preferences or conflicting 'preference maps'. Last year, I bribed a judge to fix a couple of traffic tickets, and I was glad to do so because I saved my license. Yet, at election time, I helped to vote the corrupt judge out of office. I speed on the highway; yet I want the police to enforce laws against speeding. I used to buy mixers in returnable bottles – but who can be bothered to return them? I buy only disposables now, but to soothe my conscience, I urge my state senator to outlaw one-way containers. I love my car; I hate the bus. Yet I vote for candidates who promise to tax gasoline to pay for public transportation. [. . .] I have an 'Ecology Now' sticker on a car that drips oil everywhere it's parked.[2]

By placing our faith in the markets we have gone from active participants, custodians and agents of the economic process to passive recipients of the benefits, and harms, of the industrial economy, living on a planet polluted, damaged and stripped bare of its natural bounty. By overlooking power we leave ourselves without an explanation for our planetary stalemate. We regulate companies but only half-heartedly, remaining puzzled when it seems that the market delivers not to everyone with equal generosity but almost exclusively to the already successful and the already wealthy, at the expense of our societies and ecosystems. How did we get here? Why are we so reluctant to purposefully direct the economy towards the public good? How did we become convinced that all we have to do is nothing?

The free market system is built on a modus operandi of passivity: no one has power over the system, the system itself delivers the allocation of resources truly most desired by society. This is a core tenet of free market thinking – the public good will magically materialize if we allow people and companies to selfishly pursue their own interests.

The most famous articulation of this belief can be found in Adam Smith's 'invisible hand': in spite of their natural selfishness – in fact, precisely because of it – the rich will come to share their bounty with the poor by employing them and providing them with goods and services that they can buy with their wages. The rich 'are led by an invisible hand to make nearly the same distribution of the necessaries of life which would have been made had the earth been divided into equal portions among all its inhabitants'.[3] Entirely incidentally, accidentally, the richest among us will take care of us all – and fairly, too.

'It is not from the benevolence of the butcher, the brewer, or the baker,' Smith tells us, 'that we expect our dinner, but from their regard to their own interest.'[4] The reasoning goes thus: without doing anything (in fact, by actively suppressing the urge to intervene), market forces will themselves deliver the best possible outcome. If chemical companies poison surrounding water supplies, or if the vast green stretches of central Europe are turned into biodiversity wastelands, this must somehow be for the best. Because if it was not, the market would self-correct, by itself. It is Orwellian double-think. Despite every temptation, we must not intervene, lest we miss out on the promised largesse of the market.

Smith's work was rich with insights into how free markets work, and their limitations, but it is the simplest ideas that have spread the farthest. The invisible hand logic is embedded within theories such as trickledown economics – the rising tide that floats all boats – and marginal productivity theory, which counsels that in free markets every 'factor of production', including human beings, will receive its fair reward in line with its economic contribution. Rich people, and profitable companies, are merely passive recipients of their due reward, and we all stand to benefit, indirectly, from their success and selfishness.

In fact, between them, these three notions – the invisible hand, marginal productivity and trickledown – form an unbreakable Gordian knot of mythology that fastens the restraints on public policy and cordons off the free markets from government intervention. These ideas are ostensibly based on the concepts of deservedness, fairness and public benefit, but they are really anchored in success to the successful and freedom to the same. They sit behind the notion that the private sector is efficient; the public sector is wasteful. Regulation distorts the market. People are better at spending their own money than the government. Income taxes discourage effort and cause our brightest minds to flee. We need to pay company bosses high wages and big bonuses if we want to attract the best talent. In a competitive market, only the best companies survive. Dominant companies must be more innovative or they would not be on top. These are all different ways of saying that we can trust competition, free markets can be depended upon implicitly, efficiency will prevail, that more money is always better, and wealth has no opportunity to consolidate. Society will be better off, and any social costs of free markets are worth it.

If free markets are left to run riot, it is assumed that whatever allocation the market delivers, however unequal, however imbalanced, however incomplete and inefficient it appears to be, it must be the best that can be achieved, for it comes with the market's blessing.

But the world we actually live in is replete with market failures. Whilst consumers get intangible 'utility' – supposedly swimming around in a well-provisioned world of cheap stuff – companies and those running and investing in them get cold, hard cash and, if they are able to take advantage of market failure loopholes, far more than their fair share, at our collective expense. With money comes power, the power to do more harm, to earn more money and entrench the status quo. This is efficiency, this is opportunity, this is freedom, this is justice. This is competition.

## The pristine monopolist

It is not illegal just to have a monopoly or market power. The law kicks in only if there is some kind of 'bad' act to exclude rivals and tamper with the competitive process, to raise artificial barriers to entry or block legitimate competition. The suspect act could be a merger, where it would result in unacceptable market power, or a cartel – which is when multiple firms team up to coordinate their prices or output in order to short-circuit the competition that otherwise exists between them (like Archer Daniels Midland did with lysine in the 1990s) – or it could be what is called 'monopolization' in the US, in breach of Section 2 of the Sherman Act, or 'abuse of dominant position' in the EU, which triggers Article 102 of the EC Treaty. In general, it is thought that a 'pristine monopolist', one that has reached its position of market power without evidence of exclusionary or cartel-like behaviour, should not be punished for the high prices the market will bear.

The argument is often taken even further – to maintain not just that successful monopolists should not be punished but that their presence in the market is actively beneficial because big firms bring with them scale efficiencies and because monopolists have the excess profits to invest in research and development.

Joseph Schumpeter is the economist most closely associated with the notion that monopolistic firms are good for the economy in terms of innovation. At first wary that the bureaucracy of big companies would stifle innovation, he later came to embrace large-scale enterprise as the most powerful engine of economic progress.[5] Larger firms have greater incentives and ability to invest in research and development, he said, and temporary market power is essential as a reward for innovation. Not only was perfect competition, in a market comprising many small buyers and sellers, impossible to achieve in real life, it was also inferior. Monopoly would actually lead to higher output and lower prices by virtue of innovation. In fact, according to Schumpeter, the lure of monopoly profits was needed to induce businesses to invest and innovate. The 'gales of creative destruction' will ensure continued economic dynamism as each incumbent technology is replaced by the next new disruptor. If the monopoly survives the storm, then it must deserve its position.

What is perhaps most remarkable about this view, with its implicit trust in monopolistic business, is that this theory, this pure assumption, has been firmly settled in antitrust law. In 2004, the US Supreme Court confirmed that 'The mere possession of monopoly power, and the concomitant opportunity to charge monopoly prices, is not only not unlawful; it is an important element of the free-market system. The opportunity to charge monopoly prices – at least for a short period – is what attracts business acumen in the first place.'[6] The pristine monopolist is to be applauded, not vilified.

Conjecture as to how the economy may work has become a truth guiding the belief that it must be regulated only lightly. The evidence, however, does not support Schumpeter.[7] Rather, it shows that competition can spur innovation more than monopoly, with the bursts of technological progress following the break-up of AT&T in the early 1980s being the most frequently cited example.

And, in fact, the supposed innovativeness of dominant firms is often due not to private genius and investment but to public investment in basic research – it is not the reward of profit that incentivizes innovation but the foresight and vision of government. Mariana Mazzucato has successfully debunked the image of the innovative private sector, showing that such leaps in technology as are embedded in the internet and the iPhone arose off the back of publicly funded research, given for free to the private sector to market to consumers.[8]

There are some industries, typically those involving significant research and development outlay, where limited monopoly is tolerated precisely in the hope that it will result in innovation: intellectual property rights, in essence, are a publicly granted monopoly over a particular technology for a limited time, to allow the inventor to recoup their costs and to incentivize investment in the first place. But, not content with limited monopoly, pharmaceutical firms, in particular, have found ways to extend their patent protections, or to gain the benefit of monopoly without having to innovate by buying up patents from other companies. The result is the ratcheting up of the prices of essential drugs like insulin, especially in countries with privatized medical systems. Indeed, the drive for shareholder returns actually causes firms to significantly underinvest in R&D, as they prefer instead to return cash to shareholders through dividends and share buybacks.

The Schumpeterian narrative also downplays the role of power and the possibility of the monopolist entrenching their power, buying up or eliminating their rivals, embedding their own technology in the industry, controlling the dissemination of ideas and the direction of research. The innovative monopolist, like those in the finance industry, will innovate in the direction of power and benefit to shareholders, not necessarily in the best interests of consumers or society. The gales of creative destruction may rage against the monopoly but monopolists can control the weather.

Market-dominating status, which is achieved through superior quality, lower costs and greater innovation, can be locked in by companies erecting barriers to entry, to keep new entrants out – effectively shutting the door behind them. The winner takes it all. And although neoliberals have always placed faith in the idea that the market will self-correct, it turns out that if this happens at all, it happens very, very slowly and not necessarily completely.[9] Even cartels, thought to be much less stable and harder to maintain than unilateral power grabs by a monopolist, continue to arise across many industries, with an average lifespan of eight years – which is plenty of time in which to inflict consumer and market harm. Microsoft, dominant for decades, was later joined by Apple, Amazon and Alphabet, but is still one of the most valuable companies in the world. Power persists.

## *Too big to regulate*

The market power that concerns antitrust is conceived very narrowly as the ability to raise prices and restrict output in carefully defined product markets. But true market power is the ability to act independently and without serious repercussions – independence not just from competitors and consumers but from government and society. The extra profits that are extracted from the market via higher prices can themselves form the basis of power, which can be wielded in all sorts of ways to further the company's interests, and can be distributed within the company, first and foremost to shareholders.

Clearly, there are limits to what even monopolists can do – and no monopoly lasts for ever – but in the meantime, when companies become so enormous, ubiquitous and powerful, as some appear to be today, they can move beyond the realm of public control. They determine the market; they are the market.

It is not just market power that disappeared under the assumptions of the competitive and easily contestable market. Economic and political power, including the power to influence regulation, and the power to inflict social and environmental harm, also disappeared from our models. Zephyr Teachout and Lina Khan are amongst the very few antitrust scholars linking broader corporate power to industrial concentration.[10] They liken the charging of higher-than-competitive prices to the company effectively levying a tax on the citizenry. To any one consumer it may be the difference between paying a few extra pennies for a bar of soap or a bag of sugar, but taken together it allows companies and the individuals behind those companies to amass fortunes. Market power allows them to do it and they get more power by doing so, further cementing their power.

This power manifests itself in what we can roughly categorize as 'economic power' and 'political power'. Economic power is power over the conditions of the market; it is broader than antitrust's narrow 'market power'. It may be the bargaining power of the big supermarket chain over suppliers and workers, it may be the power to squash smaller rivals and to force others to play nice.[11] Political power is the exercise of influence over the political sphere. It is the manipulation of the political process and the shaping of the regulatory system. There are clearly overlaps, but the key point is that neither currently features in how we administer competition or regulate corporate power today, and both are systematically underestimated.

## Economic power

### Power to set the standards in the market

A major industry player is able to dictate the terms of the market. For example, when Walmart decided that deodorant should no longer be sold in cardboard because the packaging added unnecessary extra cost, it had the power to impose this condition on its suppliers and soon packaging-free deodorant became the industry standard. As one commentator puts it: '[W]hole forests have not fallen in part because of the decision made in the Wal-Mart home office at the intersection of Walton Boulevard and SW 8th Street in Bentonville, Arkansas, to eliminate the box.'[12] But of course Walmart is the tenth most valuable economic entity in the world, behind just nine countries and above many more.[13] Walmart, by virtue of its size and dominance, has state-like power in the markets it operates in. Or consider Uber's commitment to help all its London drivers to transition to electric vehicles by 2025.[14] Or DuPont's strategy of accepting restrictions on the production of chlorofluorocarbons (CFCs) due to scientific concerns over harm to the ozone layer, and thus abandoning a multibillion-dollar business, but only once it had developed commercial alternatives and the profitability of producing CFCs had fallen.[15]

A private decision by a corporate entity in its own interests can have the equivalent effect to a law passed by the government. In these cases the companies were able to push the boundaries of social benefit without government intervention. But we are reliant on the public good aligning well with corporate self-interest. Walmart could also significantly restrict the sale of guns in America, if it chose to, but that would harm sales. DuPont could have acted sooner on CFCs.

Meanwhile, platform operators – like Amazon, Deliveroo and Uber – run their own internal markets and set their own rules of the game, impacting not only customers but the livelihoods of gig economy workers and individual merchants. Zero hours contracts, the industry wage and workers' rights, the path of innovation, the exploitation of financial vulnerabilities – powerful companies have the power to choose how to make their money and, in so doing, they establish the standards and practices for whole industries.

## Systemic importance

We know what happens when organizations become 'too big to fail' – lest we forget the global financial crisis. I had a front-row seat working on the string of bank and building society consolidations that were approved as part of stabilizing the British financial sector, and it was clear that some of these companies had taken on a level of national importance quite separate from their everyday commercial activities.

But this principle does not just apply to failing businesses: companies with any kind of systemic importance, integrated into the economy through supply chains and government contracts, can gain disproportionate power and become 'too big to regulate'. This is what authorities found when they considered banning Uber in London – due to safety violations – and received a petition signed by several hundreds of thousands of users united in objection. And no wonder Uber is so popular with customers – investors have been subsidizing their rides, acting on the promise that Uber would crush the competition, as it has so easily done, whilst making year on year financial losses. The investors have been hoping they will be able to exit before the vulnerabilities of the business model are revealed, and the recent IPO presented just such an opportunity.

Or think of the failed attempts by governments around the world unable to hold Mark Zuckerberg to account for the ways in which Facebook has been used as a tool to subvert democracy – he refuses to even attend most of their hearings. Or when the state loses control of the provision of public services by outsourcing to private contractors, and then finds that the balance of power has shifted to the companies, when one of the contractors goes bankrupt, jeopardizing the completion of public projects and the jobs of thousands of workers – as happened in the case of Carillion, the UK construction services company, in 2018.

Big companies can take on a life of their own and become co-dependent with the state. This was the sentiment expressed by

Charles Wilson, then president and CEO of General Motors, in 1952, during his Senate confirmation hearings as Secretary of Defense: 'What was good for our country was good for General Motors and vice versa. The difference did not exist. Our company is too big. It goes with the welfare of the country.'[16] Imagine the interdependence between the US government and one or other of Amazon or Microsoft if plans go ahead to grant a $10 billion Pentagon contract making one company responsible for handling US military data and communications around the world, this alongside plans to appoint Amazon the default platform for procurement by government agencies in the US.[17]

Even Alan Greenspan has suggested that companies that are too big to fail are too big to exist.[18] In the 1960s, Greenspan bemoaned the loss of monopolies: 'No one will ever know what new products, processes, machines, and cost-saving mergers failed to come into existence, killed by the Sherman Act before they were born.'[19] By 2009 he had changed his tune, from a monopolistic pro-lifer to firmly pro-choice, but not until after he oversaw the biggest financial catastrophe in global history as the chairman of the US Federal Reserve. And what has happened after the financial crisis? Just ten years later, the banks have convinced regulators to loosen rules designed to prevent another collapse. Their influence is undiminished.

Part of the 'too big to regulate' phenomenon is the space that these companies occupy in public debate. If someone suggests rapid decarbonization, for example, which, one way or another, is a step we cannot avoid on the path to climate stability, someone else will inevitably say, 'What about the oil companies?' or, 'It's never going to happen because of vested interests.' And something worse than actual political corruption or the exercise of overt political influence happens – we give up on the idea of taking action, without even trying. Because the oil companies do not even have to lobby, we almost do it for them by assuming that they will push in a certain direction because of their unending need for profit. It is, we shrug, just how the world works.

## Political power

### Lobbying

Market power can be leveraged into political power as companies seek to exert their influence over the political sphere.[20] One straightforward way to do this is to lobby. The drive to make regulation in Europe more efficient in the 1990s proceeded under the banner of 'Better Regulation' ('better' generally meaning 'less') and certain corporations, including British American Tobacco, played an instrumental role in lobbying for the streamlining of the regulatory process in Europe.[21] Every year, billions are spent in similar attempts to influence regulators and manipulate elections. Big Oil alone spent $1 billion in the three years following the Paris Agreement to undermine climate action.[22] Greenpeace has documented how the coal industry managed to essentially become its own regulator by co-opting the regulatory process, resulting in weaker industry standards than would otherwise have been adopted.[23]

Teachout and Khan give the example of the 2008 Farm Bill in the US to illustrate how this can work in practice. New rules proposed by the Department of Agriculture would have closely policed how meat packers and meat processors wield their market power against farmers, levelling the playing field between the world's biggest meat companies and independent farmers. So, as Teachout and Khan write, 'the meat lobby got working'. By late 2010, the National Chicken Council had commissioned a study estimating that the new rules would cost the broiler industry more than $1 billion. The National Meat Association funded research that raised the spectre of 23,000 job cuts. The American Meat Institute released an even more sensational report threatening costs of $14 billion of GDP, $1.36 billion in lost tax revenue, and 104,000 jobs. Tyson, one of the largest meat processors, submitted a 335-page legal brief, which challenged almost every element of the proposed rules, as well as the agency's authority to impose it. By the time the final rule was issued, over half of the provisions of the law had been diluted or abandoned. In separate 'poultry hearings', held around the country, many farmers did not show up to have their views heard as part of the democratic process of consultation for fear of retaliation by the companies to which they were beholden for their livelihoods. Meanwhile, studies show that, as compared to business interests, citizen groups have little or no independent influence on policy, facing insuperable hurdles to collective action.[24]

The food system, like the financial system, perhaps because it is so important, seems to be particularly susceptible to this manipulation. At the same time, the market structure amplifies corporate influence. Consolidation is taking place across the agri-food industry on a grand scale, with mega-mergers like Bayer's $66 billion buyout of Monsanto and the $130 billion merger between Dow and DuPont, covering such diverse parts of the market as seeds, agrichemicals, fertilizers, animal genetics, data and farm machinery.[25] Medical journal *The Lancet* identifies shareholder value and the political power of commercial interests as key drivers of what it calls 'The Global Syndemic' – the synergy of three connected global epidemics (obesity, undernutrition and climate change).[26] A 2019 OECD report on seed market concentration calls for changes to the intellectual property regime, removal of barriers to entry, and funding for public research.[27] These are all sensible, relatively simple ideas, so we must ask why they have not already been implemented. One reason might be that any such regulation must face the lobbying power of an industry that in the last couple of decades has concentrated down from hundreds of competitors to just four. These mega-companies have the resources to shape the industry

in their own interests, and we must pity the government officials tasked with going up against them.

There are also other less measurable, and less visible, levers of
influence than outright lobbying that companies have at their
disposal. In 2018, Facebook admitted to hiring a PR firm to
smear George Soros, a principal funder of some anti-tech cam-
paigns.[28] Google has been accused of funding research favourable
to its own preferred policy positions,[29] as well as orchestrating
and sponsoring conferences at friendly academic institutions to
which regulators are invited and introduced to pro-Google policy positions, even whilst there are ongoing investigations into
Google's conduct by those same regulators.[30] One group of
researchers was ejected from a Washington think tank because
the chairman of Google, a major funder of the institution, did
not like a press release praising the European Commission's
multibillion-dollar fines against the company.[31]

The revolving door operates in the obvious ways that it
always has,[32] with former and future regulators and politicians
landing lucrative jobs with the big firms, but there is also an
extent to which being a big, successful, prestigious company
creates almost unavoidable links with the elite: so when a US
Senator suggests that we should rely on pure self-regulation by
the tech platforms,[33] we need to bear in mind that his daughter
is a privacy manager at Facebook.[34]

### Power over market truth

Various investigations have revealed that the oil companies
knew the extent of the harm being inflicted on our planet by the
burning of fossil fuels as early as the 1970s, but they said nothing
or downplayed any evidence that did see the light of day, standing by and profiting whilst we unwittingly napalmed our future.
The same thing had happened in the tobacco industry since
the 1950s, with the major companies denying any link between

smoking and lung cancer long after they knew there to be one, continuing to recruit teenagers to enjoy their 'lifestyle product', knowing full well that the addictive properties of nicotine would give the companies a customer for life – at least until said customer's premature death. This was finally revealed by a cache of six million internal documents released as part of private litigation in the late 1990s, which told the story of decades of deception, in the companies' own words, causing the World Health Organization to investigate how its own thinking and advice had been compromised over the years by tobacco industry influence.[35]

Companies are often best placed to understand the costs of industry practices and yet they are under no obligation to share that information – and may even claim that they would be breaching duties to investors if they were to do so. We have to imagine that Google and Facebook are either themselves conducting research or are well aware of any early signs indicating the potential harms of new technologies, from AI to advanced robotics to automated vehicles. There is already evidence that the architecture of the internet, optimized for information storage and display, and designed mostly by white men, is rewiring our brains.[36] If tech companies choose to sacrifice our privacy in order to feed their AI, they can make that decision more or less unilaterally. If they knew of any threat to human society posed by the technologies they are busy developing, would they tell us? What about the agribusinesses and the impact of modern farming methods on land harvestability? Or climate change? Or pharmaceutical and health care companies and the effects of mass medicalization?

The influence over the 'market truth' is particularly important, given that this is an increasingly determinative input in regulatory decision making. Any ideological bent in academia gets magnified through the administration of law, especially when the administrators are keen to show that they are up to date with the latest theories, and academics are called as witnesses in antitrust court cases to give expert evidence on economic theories. These expert witnesses sometimes earn as much as a thousand dollars an hour.[37] Given that each side is usually able to find an economic witness to corroborate their theory of harm or benefit, one wonders if the system would be equally, or perhaps more, effective if the courts were instead to employ a non-partisan clairvoyant to assist with antitrust cases. What counts as the truth seems to be incredibly subjective.

## Power to shape the political reality

With unnerving influence over news and information, some market actors also have the power to impact the political truth. This is not just the power to lobby, it is the power to change how politics works. From the apparent manipulation of the 2016 US Presidential election to the UK's referendum on membership of the EU, Facebook in particular has the proven ability to act as a conduit for the alteration of history. In Myanmar, Facebook's content moderators failed to detect and act upon a systematic campaign of misinformation by the military to garner support for the ethnic cleansing of the Rohingya people, facilitating the genocide.[38] Twitter was similarly used to promote government propaganda covering up human rights violations against the minority Uighur people in China in 2019.[39] Google has the power to promote anti-abortion advice to women searching for an early termination facility, through misleading advertising.[40] Every single day, people around the world watch 700 million hours of videos recommended by YouTube's algorithms, which are calibrated to chase user clicks no matter how hateful or disgusting the content. The most addicted users drive the content viewed by the rest of the platform and each individual user is lured into the echo chamber of their very own filter bubble. And this power over the political and market truth is only getting stronger as local journalism is crushed by the online news machine.

Companies sometimes also have power over aspects of our personal lives that are normally within the province of the state – whereas the government will expunge any criminal record after a certain number of years, the internet never forgets, unless you fall within the EU's limited right to be forgotten. They can keep your misdeeds public but they can also make you disappear, digitally, burying your business at the bottom of search results or censuring your posts on social media. Private companies control vast repositories of the digital record of our collective past, as well as the databases on which public administrative decision making and criminal enforcement is sometimes based.

In 1937, James Landis warned that the managers of U.S. Steel and other large corporations 'possess a coercive force and effect that government even with its threat of incarceration cannot equal'.[41] It is chilling to think of the ways in which a private corporation could ruin your life if it was necessary or convenient for it to do so. By contrast, what would it take for any government, say the US government, to shut down Facebook or Google or Amazon? These companies have their own servers, many located outside the US, and there is no 'off' switch for the internet.

Of course, smaller companies may attempt all of these paths to influence. But big companies benefit from visibility, systemic importance and economies of scale from lobbying that allow them to get more political bang for their campaigning buck.[42] Google, for example, had 120 lobbying meetings with a commissioner, cabinet member or director-general of the EU between 2014 and 2016.[43] The networking effect of new technology plays its part. We can imagine that they were more successful in getting their views heard, and getting those meetings in the first place, than smaller, less economically important companies.

These examples of economic and political power show the many creative ways in which the shareholder value company will attempt to boost its profits. The simplistic focus within anti-trust on the market power of some companies to increase price misses many variants of power. Many of the tools that powerful companies have at their disposal to subvert the market or the will and norms of society are dismissed as harmless.

## Power to do harm

What is the link between competition and the negative spill-overs of corporate activities? Mainstream doctrine does not make much of a connection. If anything, a monopolist is thought to be less harmful – in raising prices and restricting output, it is assumed that the company with market power will also reduce its pollution or production of other social harms. Equally, a firm in a competitive industry will not have the power or resources to change how the market works, it is thought, whereas a monopolist is able to make changes – to produce a less harmful but more expensive product, without the fear of being undercut.

There are a few issues with this logic. Firstly, this argument is incompatible with the idea that monopolists ramp up production because they enjoy economies of scale. Cows emit methane – a powerful greenhouse gas – and whether cattle are scattered across the countryside or packed together at a big commercial farm makes little difference, so in theory a big farm is no more harmful than many small ones. But the commercial farm exists to exploit both market power and benefits of scale, and may well rear more cows to meet global demand than individual farmers would ever have dreamt of, and do so under less desirable conditions.

Second, even if the monopolist does reduce production, there is no reason to think that the level of spillovers will decrease. The company can switch to a more polluting production pro-cess or a more polluting product, and without competition the excess profits earned will not be competed away by a company offering a less polluting alternative. This is linked to the third point, which is that just because a company can afford to do good – due to excess rents extracted through market power – this does not mean that it will. In fact, which brings us to the fourth point, the company with rents to spare can use them to underwrite their externalities and to fight any litigation or regulatory punishment that may one day materialize – as DuPont did in relation to the dangerous chemicals used in Teflon production.[44] Similarly, in 2019 Facebook set aside a $3 billion allowance in its accounts for regulatory fines it could see coming down the line (the eventual negotiated fines were $5 billion), and in 2018, eight years after the Deepwater Horizon oil rig blowout, BP cleared room for $1.7 billion of liability and $2 billion of cash payouts relating to the spill, with BP's Chief Financial Officer assuring investors that such disbursements were 'fully manageable within our existing financial framework'.[45] Plenty of room on the balance sheet for disaster, with clear headroom for profit. A firm with market power and excess rents can afford to face such liability, no sweat. It is just a cost of doing business.

Companies with excess rents can use their profits to influence their regulatory environment – we have seen this in banking as, a mere ten years after global financial collapse, the financial industry is successfully lobbying for post-crisis preventative rules to be relaxed. They can push for more permissive antitrust rules and higher barriers to entry into the market, to shore up their traditional market power, but they can also lobby for lighter environmental regulation or less stringent worker protections. This will be easier to do in a monopolistic or oligopolistic industry, like global fast fashion or car manufacturing or banking, not only because there will be more profits to commit to the exercise but also because it will be easier to coordinate the single or few industry participants in the lobbying effort.

There is an empirical question of whether monopolies pollute more or produce other externalities in greater number than companies facing competition, but there has been little research into the issue – as one might expect, since the problem is assumed away by free market thinking. There is some evidence, though, that dominant firms behave differently during the phase when they are competing for monopoly than they do once their supremacy has been achieved. Facebook offered more privacy protections whilst Google was still in the social networking space, and the market was somewhat competitive, than it did once it dominated the market alone.[46]

There will be many industries that are usually characterized as highly competitive, like the auto industry, with tight margins and fierce rivalries, which are nevertheless responsible for significant pollution. But, in fact, the auto industry is an oligopoly market with just a few competing players, and they are able to coordinate with each other to increase social harm – for example, by agreeing to delay the introduction of cleaner technologies, as auto manufacturers did in California in the 1950s and possibly again in Europe more recently.[47] Other 'competitive' industries reach for externalities as a driver of profits precisely because the market will not bear higher prices and there are no barriers to entry behind which a company can protect a monopolistic position. But it is difficult to isolate an example of a market with many small buyers and sellers that has significant externalities – partly because few truly competitive markets exist in the real world (contrary to Myth #1) but also because smaller-scale producers may not have the same opportunity or incentive to degrade their product, working conditions or environment as their monopolistic, large-scale equivalents would.

## Arm wrestling with corporate power

It will be immediately obvious to anyone with a passing familiarity with the real world that no society has managed to achieve public good through invisible means alone, whatever Adam Smith argued. The regulatory government is often called upon to channel the simultaneously constructive and destructive forces of capitalism. But it is the political ideology of free markets – as distinct from the actual theory of modern economics – that dictates how seriously the free market loopholes are taken and how enthusiastically we act to minimize them. At present, they are not taken seriously enough, as policymakers stick to the mantra of free markets or bust.

Currently, companies – even big companies with huge economic importance – are still only accountable and responsible for their shareholders' interests. The havoc that this one principle wreaks on the global economy is enormous, and antitrust has played its part in allowing companies to become big with no responsibility for the inevitable consequences. Responsibility has been completely divorced from power, and vice versa. In fact, power has more or less disappeared from the discussion altogether. There are lots of levers to pull to meet the challenges ahead, but how we treat the winners of the race to dominance sets the tone for the whole system. If our biggest and most powerful companies do not have to face responsibility and share power, then no one else will.

What the free market myths are trying to deflect attention from are a few harsh truths. The initial allocation of resources, wealth, skills and talents matter – in fact, they are determinative – and thus should not be ignored. The outcomes of the market are not 'natural', they are chosen through commission or omission by society and moulded by those whom the market treats most favourably. Corporate conduct is channelled towards whatever scheme will make the most money, and then the next most, and then the next most, with scant regard for planetary, social and moral boundaries – or any other boundary, except the financial. Capital flows to where there is opportunity, and it competes and wins for itself, and there are real people – and not that many of them – who take home the dividends.

Adam Smith's 'invisible hand', which explained that it is not the benevolence but rather the self-interest of the butcher, the brewer and the baker that guides the market to its best, most efficient outcome, is just one part of the story. The invisible hand may optimize, but it does so based on the existing distribution of wealth and resources. This distribution is not random, it is a choice, and it is chosen by another, equally invisible hand. Economist Adam Ozanne is one of a handful of scholars integrating concepts of power into modern economics. As Ozanne describes:

> The first invisible hand promotes efficiency and mutually beneficial outcomes, the second works through conflict and division to promote particular outcomes that benefit some more than others. Thus, extreme levels of poverty and deprivation may persist or deepen while a powerful (and perhaps lucky and hard-working) few – such as today's bankers and hedge fund managers – receive excessive rewards and bonuses.[48]

In the words of Robert Reich, 'The invisible hand of the marketplace is connected to a wealthy and muscular arm.'[49] It cannot be said, as some still believe, that the poor deserve their lot. There are two invisible hands at work, and the second has everything to do with power. It is the second one that chooses which version of 'efficiency' we arrive at, and for whose benefit.

The free market outcome is presented as optimal, and it is assumed that no one has undeserved power. But the market price and profits delivered by the market reflect not just some existential value but rather the bargain struck between transacting parties and their relative power. Every market price has embedded within it an expression of our free market ideology: power to the powerful, success to the successful, and harm to those who are given no rights or power to protect themselves.

There has always been this fanciful idea that, of course, if the market generates unacceptable outcomes, we can regulate it externally – set the rules of the game in which free market competition can operate – and redistribute the proceeds through taxation. It is a fig leaf offered by free marketeers, but just as quickly taken away again with the insistence that the market does, after all, know best: it gives to those who are most deserving, and benefits us all indirectly, so its methods should be questioned, and outcomes recalibrated, only in extreme circumstances.

We have surely entered such a phase of extreme circumstances, but regulation and redistribution still must counter the objection that any interference with the free market violates the ultimate freedom of property and the right of a person to do with their talents and assets what they will, and good luck to them. Regulation and redistribution will always be in conflict with free markets, freedom for the successful 1 per cent, freedom for the crumb-collecting 99 per cent, and freedom in general. But as long as the second invisible hand chooses the game to be played by the first, the promised efficiency, the promised trickle of social benefit, will continue to accrue to the rich few and not the poor many. Meanwhile, power consolidates: the power to increase the market price, yes, but also the power to control the whole market, determine the boundaries of the market, who gets to play, who does not, and who stands to benefit.

As George Monbiot writes, 'The freedom that neoliberalism offers, which sounds so beguiling when expressed in general terms, turns out to mean freedom for the pike, not for the minnows' – the big fish flourish whilst the little fish get eaten.

He adds that:

Freedom from trade unions and collective bargaining means the freedom to suppress wages. Freedom from regulation means the freedom to poison rivers, endanger workers, charge iniquitous rates of interest and design exotic financial instruments. Freedom from tax means freedom from the distribution of wealth that lifts people out of poverty.[50]

As the neoliberal view captured the intellectual stage, and the state has receded, this freedom has meant freedom for the shareholder and consumer to vote with their wallets, but increasingly fewer opportunities for unmoneyed citizens to vote through government.

As with the recognition that free markets are not really competitive, we may need to step up our regulation of corporate power to take account of not only the many forms of corporate power that permeate the market but also to counter the attempts by corporations to avoid or undermine other regulation – from environmental law and workers' rights to tax law and financial regulation. To the extent that there will always be some corporate power – the corporation is a naturally powerful vehicle – that power should be shared more evenly, so that it does not merely serve the interests of the already powerful. Our passive trust in big, powerful companies has been abused. Active participation in determining our own futures is the only solution.

---

**SUMMARY**

**Myth #3:** Corporate power is benign.

**Reality:** There are many types of corporate power that allow the powerful to choose how to shape the economy and society in their interests.

# 4.

# *Anti-what now?*

Myth #4: We already control corporate power with antitrust

In 1882, oil magnate John D. Rockefeller formed the Standard Oil Trust, and began to buy up the US oil industry, eventually bringing under its organizational umbrella 90 per cent of the oil production in America. This stimulated a raft of copy-cat arrangements in sugar, whisky, lead, rope, cottonseed oil and linseed oil by industrialists nicknamed the 'robber barons'.[1] Standard Oil engaged in a torrid menu of unfair dealings to secure its supremacy, including agreeing with the railroads to raise the cost of carriage for rivals, intimidating smaller firms into selling out to the trust with the threat of ruination, and bearing down its political influence over the whole industry in the grant or obstruction of new pipelines.

At the same time, mass production and mass distribution introduced a new conflict into political discourse. The concentration of power was disturbing, but the scale of production that it allowed brought about a level of national industriousness that was hard to resist. Americans were propelling these behemoths forward with their eager consumption, although many continued to be troubled by the question of what economic and political life under the dominion of such companies would be like.[2] What was the price that would be paid for industrial progress?

Now, unlike in the past, an international force of antitrust regulators steward the development of industry and, in theory, watch specifically for the impairment of competition, dominance in markets and aggregations of power. You would think that antitrust lawyers, regulators and economists would be very sensitive to signs of growing market power, perhaps even overzealous, trained as they are to spot market distortions in their incipiency. If that were the case, any industrial concentration that we see, and the accompanying harms, must have been regulator-approved and is therefore nothing to worry about.

And yet the evolution of antitrust has plotted a very different path to what you might expect, a path which has failed to keep up with accelerating industrial consolidation. Antitrust has turned into a technocratic field of experts mechanistically applying dated economic theories, out of touch with the urgent reality of our times. These enforcers earnestly review mergers and other corporate schemes designed to avoid competition and to consolidate power, but generally deem that they are benign or beneficial, bewitched by theories that convince them this is so. I saw this at first hand when representing big corporations before the antitrust authorities, as well as when I switched sides to work for government enforcers reviewing corporate power. Almost all mergers are cleared by the authorities, and few monopolists are challenged. And what started out as an American preoccupation with neoclassical economics, consumer welfare, price and the infallibility of markets, has been replicated in the EU, and across the world. Antitrust has become a merely mythological constraint on corporate power.

## Must bust trust

The US Sherman Act of 1890, which was eventually used to break up the Standard Oil Trust in 1911, is often treated as the foundational antitrust statute. Indeed, the word 'antitrust' comes from the original motivation of the legislation – to break up industry consolidations that had used the legal 'trust' structure to ward off regulation – hence anti-*trust*.*

Antitrust law was a response to the power of the trusts, but the trusts had developed as a way to circumvent a different regulatory device taking aim at their scope.[3] Before the Sherman Act, corporate power in the US had been controlled not by the federal government but by individual states. Companies have always relied upon the government for the right to incorporate – it is the government that grants companies the ability to become companies – so individual American states had used this leverage to control corporate activities through corporate law: by prohibiting corporations from doing business outside the incorporating state, or prohibiting one company from owning shares in another, and thus placing inbuilt limits on the scale of industry.[4]

As the US national market grew and became more interconnected, companies were able to choose in which state to register, and the powerful trusts were able to lobby for weakened incorporation laws – which some states were happy to provide in order to attract companies and the associated registration fees and tax revenues. Corporate law was no longer an effective limit on corporate power.

The Sherman Act, a federal antitrust statute sitting above state incorporation laws, was supposed to step into this regulatory gap, but it was a weaker tool for containing corporate power than state corporate laws had been. Corporate law empowered states to sue if a company breached the terms of its licence, with a

---

*Trusts started out with a technical, legal meaning – referring to the consolidation of various market rivals under a single legal 'trust' structure, overseen by trustees instead of boards of directors. Eventually, 'trusts' came to be synonymous with 'big business', and 'antitrust' with the regulatory response to such businesses. See also the Glossary at the back of the book for more on the definition of 'antitrust'.

presumption of harm to the public interest, on the basis that incorporation is a privilege which the state is empowered to take away. But instead of following this model for the regulation of corporate power in federal antitrust, the drafters of the Sherman Act based the legislation on the common law principle of 'restraint of trade', which was not designed as a curb on power per se.

Unlike corporate law, which could punish a breach of corporate duties with the dissolution of the company, threatening the very existence of the powerful corporation, the common law concepts of restraint of trade and monopolization permitted reasonable distortions of competition.[5] The possibility of a justifiable monopoly was always left open, and the courts were more willing to step in where there was clear evidence that dominance had been achieved through illegal acts, directly restricting competition, rather than through the merit of the 'pristine monopolist' – a high bar. The government could not go after the broad basis of power and instead had to pick away at individual corporate acts in a piecemeal fashion, in each case showing some anti-competitive economic harm.[6]

Whilst the shape of modern antitrust was crystallizing in the form of 'restraint of trade' under the Sherman Act, some, like Supreme Court Justice Louis Brandeis, argued that focusing on economic harm was a red herring – the problem was not monopoly as such but rather the sheer bigness of these conglomerate enterprises. Brandeis lamented the 'curse of bigness'[7] and argued that it was necessary to '[curb] physically the strong, to protect those physically weaker' in order to sustain industrial liberty.[8] As Brandeis is famously supposed to have said, 'We must make our choice. We may have democracy, or we may have wealth concentrated in the hands of a few, but we can't have both.'* Bigness posed a fundamental threat to economic

* In fact, the source of this quote is much debated and it is possibly apocryphal, but it is famous nonetheless.

democracy, he argued. But this was not the concern that was ultimately embedded within the Sherman Act, and mimicked in competition laws across the world. Antitrust, unlike corporate law, would limit itself to prosecuting only economically harmful monopolies and not corporate power more broadly.

## *All hail, neoliberalism!*

The University of Chicago became the gravitational centre of neoliberal thinking in the twentieth century, grabbing hold of the view that markets should be left free, companies should serve only shareholders, and monopolists should not be heavily regulated. But in fact the early Chicagoans – what we might call Chicago School Mark I – in the 1930s had been more in tune with Brandeis. They had been concerned with corporate power as a threat to economic freedom, and saw monopoly as the enemy of democracy.

One scholar and founding member of the Chicago School, Henry Simons, called for the 'outright dismantling of . . . gigantic corporations' and the 'persistent persecution' of producers with market power.[9] He thought antitrust violations should be 'prosecuted unremittingly by a vigilant administrative body'. Even Milton Friedman initially supported the government's role in cracking down on monopoly power – it was for the state to 'police the system' of the competitive order, he wrote, and to 'establish the conditions favorable to competition and prevent monopoly'.[10]

This pro-enforcement view did not last, however, particularly once the government started acting upon it. Concerns with economic power were soon replaced wholesale by an abiding distrust of the power of the state.

The free market agenda at Chicago was initially driven by an outsider from Europe – Austrian economist Friedrich Hayek. He feared the rising power of the interventionist post-war state, having seen in Germany what could happen when a fascist leader gets control of highly monopolized and concentrated industry, and the concurrent ability of a highly monopolized industry to bring their chosen leader to power. This is what conglomerates like chemicals company I.G. Farben had done, and the executives of the company were later tried for war crimes and crimes against humanity at Nuremberg, having manufactured the gas used by the Nazis to kill millions of Jews.[11]

Unlike Brandeis, for Hayek the solution was not to make sure there are no monopolies for a fascist leader to take hold of – he instead wanted to make sure that the government would always be too small and too weak, relative to private enterprise, to usurp private power. Hayek saw 'in the encroachment of state intervention on every aspect of social and economic life', as he characterized the New Deal and British welfare state, 'a creep-ing totalitarianism'.[12] Whereas others thought it would be possible to stave off communism by taming free markets, Hayek saw the development of socialism by stealth. Socializing capital-ism would be the death of it, he feared.

Fundamentally, Hayek saw himself as a champion for free-dom – but it was freedom for private property, for the ruthless monopolist, for the wealthy and the successful. Friedman too exalted shareholder value on the same basis, arguing that com-petitors should be left free as long as they stuck to the 'rules of the game', by which he meant 'free competition'. But by the 1970s the 'rules of the game' had come to mean competition between monopolies who were assumed to act 'as if' they constantly faced the threat of the disruptive upstart.

After the Second World War, Hayek in particular could see that the Cold War would be won through a battle of ideas.[13] Ironically borrowing from the playbook of the Fabian socialists who had founded his home academic institution – the London School of Economics – Hayek formed the Mont Pelerin Society in 1947 as a free marketeers' AA meeting where the goal is not to cure yourself but convert everyone else.[14] The objective was to formulate a strategy to rescue the liberal economic order.

The phoenix that rose from the intellectual ashes of market liberalism at Mont Pelerin, and eventually found its home at the University of Chicago, was Chicago School Mark II, new liberalism, or 'neoliberalism', which took a fresh approach towards economic power (effectively denying that it exists) and individual freedom (holding it as supreme). Whilst those on the left thought the continued growth of corporations would at some point overpower the state, and that companies should therefore be nationalized or brought within state control, neoliberal Chicago antitrust became synonymous with self-correcting markets, benign corporate expansion and transient market power. Indeed, if monopoly persists, it was thought to be through the fault of government not the markets.

Mark II Chicagoans came to think that any government intervention in the market was a fundamental, proto-fascistic breach of individual freedom. These ideas were not taken seriously at first, belonging to what jurist Richard Posner, himself a Chicagoan, later described as the 'lunatic fringe' of academia.[15] But after a time, this faith in free markets, the conviction that market power can always be tamed by competition, that companies will pass on their cost savings to consumers and that the most efficient scenario will necessarily crystallize, as if according to some natural law à la Adam Smith's invisible hand, led to an ideological bias towards big companies that came to overwhelm the animating goals of antitrust and any former disquiet over power. Even their love of the ideal of perfect competition could not convince these conservatives of the need for government intervention to protect it. For Hayek this could only irreversibly lead towards socialism, repression of liberty and the degradation of the human spirit. There remained a central concern with freedom – but it was freedom for the pike, not the minnow.

## *Bork's big business bias*

Although it may seem from this brief glance at history that the antitrust enterprise was doomed from the outset, hobbled by an inability to go after power directly and by a rising ideology more sceptical of government power than of corporate abuse, actually the concept of economic harm is broad enough to have captured all sorts of different kinds of corporate power. How did antitrust come to focus on market power and price only? And how did this idea end up serving big business?

The logic flows directly from the idea that corporate muscle is a buffer against government power, as well as a conduit for low prices for consumers and a manifestation of efficiency. Prices, as a result, became almost the sole concern within antitrust.

The most influential articulation of this price-centric approach came from the pen of free market ideologue Robert Bork, whose 1978 book *The Antitrust Paradox* is still considered the seminal text of the modern antitrust era. Bork was disdainful of what he saw as the constant meddling with markets by authorities who were often doing more harm than good by inhibiting efficiency. As Bork saw it, the paradox of antitrust was that antitrust authorities sought to preserve competition by interfering with it and by protecting what he thought of as inefficient competitors. He thus labelled antitrust 'a policy at war with itself' (the subtitle of his book).

For Bork, competition was not about the process of rivalry between many firms, as most of us commonly understand it to be. Rather, competition was about an outcome: maximizing 'consumer welfare', as measured by looking at the impact of any given conduct on price. Bork argued that 'competition' was just a shorthand for whatever it was that maximized consumer welfare, which means that as long as you can characterize a market as competitive, even if there are only a few companies left competing, then you have an argument against antitrust enforcement. Bork was not the first to introduce the concept of 'consumer welfare'; he was borrowing from the toolbox of neoclassical economics. But once this cuckoo made a bed in the antitrust nest, the bias towards big business was bound to hatch.

This, in fact, was a fundamental shift – and Bork's ultimate coup. Corporate law, as we have seen, had focused on the *power* of the corporation. Restraint of trade under the Sherman Act shifted this to the *conduct* of the firm. By placing the emphasis on consumer welfare – an *outcome* – Bork put to the side the idea that we might value competitive rivalry for its own sake, that we might want to challenge power itself purely on grounds of economic imbalance or corruption, regardless of efficiency.[16] If the goal is dispersal of power, you may need to cut down big entities or introduce new firms into the market. But if the goal is efficiency, this could theoretically be achieved even through monopoly, as long as prices are low – which, handily, Bork always assumed them to be.

It is not only power that was removed from the equation. Anything that could be considered as external to the market – the subversion of democracy, a rise in inequality, pollution – was similarly minimized. These issues are not deemed to matter to consumers – if they did, the consumer would pay to be rid of them.

Bork subscribed to the myth that companies are inherently efficient (Myth #2), and big companies doubly so, because they are able to achieve 'economies of scale' – cost savings per unit, resulting from having large-scale operations, like being able to buy or produce in bulk. Zooming in on the welfare of consumers naturally drew attention away from the power of such companies and its potential harm (Myth #3). The transfers between your pocket and the monopolist disappear on this analysis, and so too does the monopolist's attempts to use the additional profits to shore up its power.

For thinkers like Robert Bork, monopoly power was either fleeting or justified – either the monopolist was the most efficient firm or its monopoly profits would be competed away by new entrants to the market. It is on the basis of these presumed efficiencies that mergers are given the go-ahead, monopolies are excused and any concern with bigness melts away. But viewed through the lens of shareholder value, and the duty to maximize returns for shareholders, it becomes less believable that efficiencies will be passed on to consumers, because they are, in fact, earmarked within the company structure for shareholders.

Bork established what is today the gold standard of competition law – the 'consumer welfare' test. But under this test, whatever happened in big companies was assumed to be good.[17] The powerful deserve their power and, somehow, in ways not clearly articulated, this situation was assumed, invisibly, to also serve the powerless. Meanwhile, the shareholders of monopolistic companies, and other powerful individuals, receded quietly into the background.

For decades, this thinking has shaped competition law enforcement (or lack of enforcement) in favour of big companies. Enforcers, lawyers, economists – even companies – are kept busy going through the motions, as if we are vigilantly taking corporate power to task. But it is just a mirage. It is as if the antitrust community donned a pair of anti-competition infrared goggles but switched the detection mode from 'power' to 'price'. The law, as critic Tim Wu remarks, has 'grown ambivalent' towards monopoly, and 'sometimes even celebrates the monopolist – as if the "anti" in "antitrust" has been discarded'.[18] Or as antitrust advocate Lina Khan writes: the 'suspicion of concentrated power is replaced with reverence for it'.[19]

What has for decades obscured this ideological bias from general scrutiny is the purposefully confusing and misleading language Bork used to describe this neoliberal antitrust.[20] Against the backdrop of rising consumerism, as people were called upon to express themselves not just in the ballot boxes as citizens but also at the checkout as consumers, Bork's labelling of his pro-corporation, pro-big business brand of antitrust as supportive of *'consumer* welfare' decisively removed any residual concern with corporate power from the antitrust agenda. The public interest would no longer feature directly in antitrust analysis, in a serious way, for it was assumed to be captured through consumer welfare and the efficiency of the market.

## *Meanwhile, back in Europe . . .*

Hayek, a European, had a huge impact on how antitrust would evolve in the US. Eventually, that influence would boomerang back to Europe, only a couple of decades later. It is generally understood that, when it comes to antitrust, things are done differently in Europe (it is even called something different outside the US: 'competition law' as opposed to antitrust). The European competition project has very different origins to the US antitrust legislation. In the US, the Sherman Act was adopted amidst a battle for power between citizens and business, and the conflicts inherent in curtailing business dominance. The competition laws in Europe, by stark contrast, were adopted as part of developing the European single market, and thus have the integration project at their heart, giving greater prominence to issues of fairness and responsibility.

The attitude to competition in the EU was also initially shaped by a rival school of thought to the neoliberals: the German 'ordoliberal' school. Whereas neoliberals held faith in the invisible hand of the free market, the ordoliberals believed in the need for a strong government to create a framework of rules to order the economy, including strong antitrust to contain corporate power. The Freiburg School of ordoliberalism was suspicious of both unrestrained private power – the monopolies and cartels that had characterized Nazi Germany – as well as of unrestrained public power.

But the neoliberal influence of the Chicago School has been discernible in EU competition policy at least since the 1990s,[21] when then Competition Commissioner Mario Monti, the first economist to be appointed to that role, imported the consumer welfare approach into EU competition law and created the office of the Chief Economist within Europe's competition regulator.* In 2001 he declared: '[T]he goal of competition policy, in all its aspects, is to protect consumer welfare by maintaining a high degree of competition in the common market.'[22] Vice-President Almunia said in 2010: '[A]ll of us here today know very well what our ultimate objective is: competition policy is a tool at the service of consumers. Consumer welfare is at the heart of our policy and its achievement drives our priorities and guides our decisions.'[23]

As we shall see, the EU Treaties can be interpreted much more broadly than this, but practitioners in Europe have generally adopted the narrower, Chicagoan view.[24] In Europe this has come to be known as the adoption of a 'more economic approach' to competition enforcement, but this unassuming phrase belies the revolution that took place under the surface of EU competition law, in which fairness – previously a core principle of the law – was substantially jettisoned in favour of economic efficiency.[25]

---

* The EU courts have actually consistently stated that the goal of EU competition law is to protect not consumer welfare but 'competition' – although in practice it can amount to the same thing because restrictions on 'competition' are adjudicated based on their predicted or actual impact on price and on consumers.

## Anti-cooperation

Despite having an established legal framework tailored to rooting out anti-competitive behaviour, corporate power continues to elude us. We have seen how the framework has changed from the original – more effective – corporate law model, and how the Chicago School altered and diluted the interpretation of the 'restraint of trade' principle, enfeebling antitrust enforcement with an oxymoronic bias towards the interests of big business.

The global competition authorities remain extremely busy, but many cases that should be brought are not, and some that should not be prosecuted are. In the former category, few challenges to vertical mergers – between suppliers, manufacturers and distributors at different levels of the supply chain – are brought, on the assumption by the authorities that such arrangements reduce Coasian 'transaction costs' and are thus beneficial, even if they create a risk of competitors getting locked out of distribution channels or losing access to critical suppliers. The Hollywood 'Studio System' of movie production, with vertically integrated movie studios, film writers and producers, distributors, cinemas and even actors, was once broken up in the 1940s but now seems to be back in the form of Netflix Originals and Amazon Prime Video.

Whilst mergers between horizontal rivals at the same level in the supply chain are challenged, this is often only once the market has consolidated down to four, three or two players already. Other big companies often bring complaints that trigger investigation of some industry tie-ups and monopolistic practices, but workers and smaller suppliers have rarely been protected from market power wielded against them.* Powerful employers, for example, can depress the wages of workers, like in a town where

---

* The market power of a buyer, as opposed to a seller, is known as 'monopsony power'.

almost all low-skilled jobs are at the one big grocery store or factory, but this kind of power has not featured particularly in antitrust reviews. By one estimate, monopsony power reduces output and employment in the US economy by 13 per cent and reduces labour's share of national income by 22 per cent.[26] Although the UK Competition and Markets Authority ultimately blocked the acquisition of Walmart-owned Asda by rival grocery chain Sainsbury's, the authority explicitly stated that the possible impact of the merger on the thousands of retail employees of the two companies would not be a factor in its assessment.[27]

This concentration of buying power hits the poorest workers hardest, and they are the least empowered to persuade the competition authorities to act. One of the most insidious examples of buyer power is the practice of tying workers to non-compete clauses so they cannot go to work for a competitor if they quit. Similarly, McDonald's was challenged for imposing 'no poach' clauses on its franchisees, effectively preventing a worker from leaving one McDonald's for a higher paying job at another McDonald's.

But the grand irony of modern antitrust enforcement is shown best through its treatment of excessive prices. Despite the prima facie obsession with prices and harm to consumers, competition law is loath to intervene to protect consumers from high prices directly. Competition law will, somewhat reluctantly, act to increase competition in a market in the hope that low prices will follow. But even though the textbook case against the monopolist is the charging of higher prices to consumers and the lowering of product quality, very few cases are brought against exploitative practices like this. High consumer prices, employment contracts with forced arbitration clauses,[28] the extraction of excessive data by online platforms – these transgressions mostly go unchallenged.

At the same time as going easy on big businesses, in recent years the authorities have been accused of targeting the little guys, prioritizing cases against consortia of piano teachers, ice skating coaches, and church organ players, whilst allowing the biggest companies to get bigger and bigger through voracious merger sprees.[29] So, instead of cracking down on Uber's bargaining power against its workers, and its dubious tactics to dominate local markets by ignoring local regulations, the US antitrust agencies have instead turned against the drivers, siding with the Seattle Chamber of Commerce's argument that, in granting drivers the right to collectively bargain, the City of Seattle had facilitated a cartel.[30]

The authorities have also been targeting other forms of cooperation, even where the goal of the agreement has been to foster sustainability or pro-social outcomes. One such arrangement was an agreement between several Dutch energy companies to accelerate the decommissioning of five coal power plants which accounted for approximately 10 per cent of the Dutch generating capacity. The Dutch competition authority – known as the ACM – stated that closing down the power plants would raise energy prices and therefore harm consumers, and maintained that the environmental benefits of the agreement were insufficient to offset the harm.[31] In particular, whilst the world at large would enjoy cleaner air, it would be Dutch consumers who would pay the price of higher energy costs.

Another notable Dutch case is known as the 'Chicken of Tomorrow'.[32] The case involved Dutch supermarkets, chicken farmers and chicken meat processors, who responded to a public outcry against the poor living conditions of chickens in factory farms by making arrangements to sell chicken meat produced under enhanced animal welfare conditions. Critically it was agreed that supermarkets should remove regular chicken meat from their shelves – a measure designed to push consumers into purchasing higher welfare chicken and to limit competition from regular chicken. The prices of happier chickens would be higher, but the critical question was: would the trade-off be worth it to consumers? As part of its investigation the ACM used consumer surveys to establish the monetary value of animal welfare, determining that some customers were willing to pay more for higher welfare chickens (up to €0.82 extra, per kg) but that the costs of the system would exceed that (the price increase was predicted to be €1.46/kg). The ACM would not approve the scheme.[33]

What is perhaps most odd about these sustainability cases is that the competition authorities find themselves in the position of blocking agreements, according to the current understanding of the law, that we can imagine not only being permitted but actually being required in the very near future. Of course it would be simpler for the government to just prescribe higher welfare chicken and to decommission coal plants, and this would be going through the proper political channels instead of requiring the competition agency to do it through the back door. But the competition authorities in these cases are not requiring anyone to do anything, they are cracking down on those who took the initiative themselves.

The aspects of the agreements that the agencies object to are the price-fixing, competition-limiting arrangements, but these tend to be necessary to limit the first-mover disadvantage that comes from doing good on your own when your competitors are eager to undercut you. This is the rationale for mandatory minimum wages – many well-meaning employers would like to pay their employees decently, but until everyone is forced to do so they would find it hard to sustain their business. They could instead form an agreement with their competitors to raise prices to accommodate higher wages, but that would be illegal – criminally so, in some jurisdictions. And yet once minimum wage laws come in, it is not only encouraged but legally required.

Companies say that the competition rules prevent or discourage them from engaging in more sustainability initiatives that require some element of cooperation with competitors. Some argue that this is just a convenient excuse – that if companies really wanted to transition to sustainable business practices, they would find a legally compliant way to do it. But even if this is the case, competition law, as it is currently enforced, provides this convenient excuse, as authorities' resources are tied up going after even this benign or positive cooperation when it happens.

Antitrust, under the old corporate law model, tied corporate power to corporate responsibility through the company's charter. These sustainability cases are at the fringe of modern competition law but they speak to the heart of the matter – the tension sitting within the discipline. What kind of behaviour do we expect from corporate citizens, and is competition law encouraging or discouraging it?

## Handcuffing the cops

The overall theme of modern competition law, following Bork, has been non-intervention: leave the markets alone and they will self-correct, should market power arise. Over the last few decades, antitrust agencies have overseen an enormous wave of consolidation across a growing number of sectors including farming, healthcare, media, publishing, advertising and pharmaceuticals.[34] Today, in the US alone, there are around 14,000 mergers per year, that is almost 40 a day, as opposed to 2,000 a year in 1980, more like 5 a day.[35]

Businesses seeking more power face a friendly system of regulation, with almost 90 per cent of mergers closing with little or no regulatory hold-up, and most of the remaining 10 per cent failing mostly due to managerial cold feet.[36] Very few deals are blocked. In America, the regulators asked for more information in only 45 out of 2,111 reported mergers in 2018.[37] Only 39 were actually challenged, of which 20 cases were settled and 9 abandoned. The European Commission also clears the overwhelming majority of deals without conditions. Between 1990 and 2019 the European Commission rendered over 7,000 merger decisions, blocking only 30 – less than 0.05 per cent of deals.[38] It is not that the regulators have been negligent – they are restrained by the web of free market myths that have found their way into the prevailing interpretation of the law. The regulators represent the silent, but busy, mouthpiece of society that has only recently begun to find its voice.

Merger activity in the tech sector is one example. The tech behemoths have between them acquired a jaw-dropping 400 companies over the last decade,[39] including some transactions that should really have raised more alarm bells, like the acquisition by Google of its main competitors in advertising (AdMob and DoubleClick), in video (YouTube), in maps (Waze); the snapping up of Instagram by Facebook (deemed not to be a competitor because picture-taking functionality was not considered important to monetization, and Instagram wasn't deemed to be a social network) and of WhatsApp; and the absorption by Amazon of Zappos, Soap.com and Whole Foods Market. The authorities barely batted an eyelid at the time.

As critic Tim Wu has commented: 'It takes many years of training to reach conclusions this absurd. A teenager could have told you that Facebook and Instagram were competitors – after all, teenagers were the ones who were switching platforms.'[40] It is only under the narrow Chicago School view that it is possible to ignore the obvious – that Instagram posed an existential threat to Facebook, as Facebook itself was well aware.

The focus on price is part of the mischief. The prices offered by these firms are, on the face of it, either very low or non-existent. It can therefore be a tough case to make that these innovative, cutting-edge, market-leading companies are anything but good for the consumer and for the economy. This is how companies like Amazon, according to critic Lina Khan, with 'missionary zeal for consumers' have 'marched toward monopoly by singing the tune of contemporary antitrust'.[41]

The causal link between the lax enforcement by the antitrust regulators and the growing levels of industry concentration remains contested – with other factors such as globalization and technological change also driving consolidation. But regardless of the origins of market power, it is the role of antitrust to shape how such consolidation emerges and manifests itself, and the enforcement agencies have been hampered from truly serving the public or even the consumer interest by the myth that competition will bubble up spontaneously, without assistance, and power will not be able to subvert it.[42]

The role of big companies in shaping our current industrial landscape is perhaps obvious, but the role of the regulators themselves, and the theories of regulation that they have applied, has been underappreciated. Whilst no one was watching, corporate regulation flipped 180° from combating corporate power to acquiescing to it. Meanwhile, the responsibilities of big companies were reduced to a responsibility to compete to make as much money as possible, with a strong prevailing faith that low prices would automatically appear, despite rising levels of concentration.

For a long-ignored discipline, antitrust has had a disproportionate impact on the state of the global economy. Now people are asking how this could have happened, and what antitrust can do about inequality and protecting democracy and privacy. It is as if there has been a program running in the background of our operating system, and a bug in the code allowed the different bits of software to grow bigger and bigger and consume more and more memory and computing resources. Our vital systems have started crashing so we have finally woken up to the need to reboot. But first we must update our virus detection software and relearn how to see a problem we have forgotten how to diagnose.

## *Power in antitrust*

'The central values of civilisation are in danger,' one paper reads. It continues:

> Over large stretches of the Earth's surface the essential condi-
> tions of human dignity and freedom have already disappeared.
> In others they are under constant menace from the development
> of current tendencies of policy. The position of the individual
> and the voluntary group are progressively undermined by exten-
> sions of arbitrary power.[43]

This is from the founding document of the Mont Pelerin Society, in 1947, and it warned of unrestrained state power. But it is a
description that could well apply today – against corporations,
not governments.

By 1993, in the new introduction to the second edition of *The
Antitrust Paradox*, Bork welcomed the early signs of the success
of his anti-antitrust campaign. Bork and others effectively
rewrote the antitrust laws without touching a statute, and without the messy business of legislating, by influencing the
evolution of judge-made law, the interpretation of that law, and
by crippling the right of private parties to enforce it.

It may seem strange, given the economists' usual reverence
for the ideal of perfect competition and the price system, that
a policy designed to enforce competition and remove market
distortions came to be so loathed by economists and, turning
the world upside down, monopoly so lionized. This change
did not come about due to some scientific breakthrough in the
economic discipline – although this was how it was sometimes presented by Bork and his colleagues. Instead, funded
by generous corporate sponsors, the Chicago School was
transformed into a mouthpiece for pro-monopoly interests,
and many of its members would go on to win Nobel prizes for

their contributions towards building the intellectual framework in which the invisible hand could happily operate for decades after.

Chicago Antitrust, from its inception, was orchestrated to protect particular interests. Friedrich Hayek coordinated the foundation of two key projects at Chicago University in the late 1940s and early 1950s – the 'Free Market Study' and the 'Antitrust Project', of which Bork was a part – both of which were funded by the William Volker Fund, the charitable arm of a national furniture distribution company and window shade manufacturer, located in Kansas City, Missouri.[44] The president of the company – Harold Luhnow – is mostly unknown, even in antitrust circles, but it was his single-minded focus that led to the establishment of the Chicago School.

Between Hayek and Luhnow's persistence, the Volker Fund's financial assistance, and Friedman's tireless promotion of free market ideals, the Chicago School was able to capture the attention of policymakers in the 1970s, desperate to fix lagging economic performance, and national leaders, especially Ronald Reagan and Margaret Thatcher, in the 1980s. These politicians implemented and disseminated the neoliberal world vision. Friedman clung to these ideas until the end. A few years before he died, he said, 'I have gradually come to the conclusion that antitrust does far more harm than good and that we would be better off if we didn't have it at all, if we could get rid of it.'[45] Antitrust has been so handicapped by the ideology of Bork and his allies that we might as well have.

Antitrust was originally broadly conceived as the challenge to big and powerful business for the threat it posed to economic and political democracy. If we are to return to more robust enforcement, we must certainly expand our notion of harm beyond the adopted concepts of efficiency and consumer welfare. But we can also confront corporate power at a fundamental level – limiting the scope of the corporation, imposing

responsibilities so that its power is wielded for the public benefit, and ultimately revoking the privilege of incorporation for
companies that stray beyond the bounds of public control and
public interest.

It is now clearer than ever that monopolistic companies set
not just the prices in their markets but the trajectory of innovation and the balance of social harm and benefit. We may not be
able to fully wind back the concentration, but it is high time to
bring antitrust back in line with our new social, environmental
and political reality and to face head on, and without flinching,
the true power of corporate interests. In doing so we may bear
in mind the ominous warning of Norbert Wiener, in 1948:

> Whether we entrust our decisions to machines of metal, or to
> those machines of flesh and blood which are . . . corporations, we
> shall never receive the right answers . . . unless we ask the right
> questions . . . [T]he hour is very late, and the choice of good and
> evil knocks on our door.[46]

---

**SUMMARY**

**Myth #4:** We already control corporate power with antitrust.

**Reality:** Modern antitrust condones corporate power.

---

# Shareholders above the law

Myth #5: The law requires companies to maximize financial
value for shareholders

Shareholders are very clear on their rights – which are strong –
and their responsibilities – which are minimal. Viewed from the
outside, this can lead to disjointed behaviour: on the one hand,
in 2005, over 48,000 investors in the company Railtrack, out-
raged by the decline in the value of their shares, clubbed together
to raise over £4 million to challenge the British Secretary of
State for Transport's decision to force the company into administration, going so far as to allege a breach of their human rights.[1]
On the other hand, at the very same time, a judgment was
handed down on Railtrack's liability in relation to a fatal train
crash, implicating the company's poor safety record and working practices. The shareholders did not feel moved to campaign
on this issue, seeing themselves as completely removed from
responsibility and viewing corporate liability as completely
unconnected to their rights as shareholders. When the value of
their shares was not maintained, it was a breach of their human
rights. When lives were lost in connection with their profit-
making, their humanity was nowhere to be found.

Even if we can dispatch the idea that free markets are competitive (Myth #1) and that companies serve the public interest
by competing (Myth #2), that corporate power is benign (Myth

#3) and that antitrust already controls harmful corporate power (Myth #4), we are left with the very problematic idea that maximizing financial value for shareholders is the law. But why? Where is this statute or legal case that says that company directors must maximize the share price, no matter what? This is not what the law says at all, and yet it is what companies feel obliged to do. How does this misunderstanding persist?

## *The inflammable company*

When it began to be widely used as a form of business organization, the corporation was the subject of considerable suspicion. It was a peculiar entity: not a partnership of real human beings but an artificial legal construct, and the shareholders behind it came to be shielded from all personal liability.

This is not how the corporation started out. The original norm of accountability was not actually limited liability but *unlimited* liability. The corporation was not a vessel for Coasian efficiency in the sixteenth century but rather a vehicle for personal responsibility. But avoiding liability was a critical part of the evolution of the corporation and is what made it so popular. Limited liability drives companies to think more ambitiously about their scope for mischief and risk. Imagine if the shareholders of oil companies were responsible for their collective contribution to climate change? Limited liability removes true responsibility and accountability. As one commentator writes, limited liability 'institutionalises irresponsibility',[2] and supercharges the basest instincts of the company. It is like giving a flamethrower to a pyromaniac. For shareholders there need be no concern: it is all upside.

As we have it today, shareholder value obliges directors to maximize returns whilst limited liability allows them to use all means necessary to shift costs out on to society without risk to shareholders. But the early corporations had a much wider scope of responsibility, as we have already seen – their very existence was subject to government decree.

Some of the first corporations were formed in England under charter by the King or Queen and they existed for a specified purpose. We talk now about a company having a 'licence to operate', based on the social contract struck between business and wider society. Originally, however, these were literal licences, granted by the sovereign. Corporate responsibility was a given: the purpose of any given corporation was defined by its charter in very practical terms – the responsibility to complete some particular public works – and its licence to operate flowed from that charter.

When capital was in short supply, the corporation was seen as a way to outsource the completion of certain public projects, from the imperialistic voyages of the Honourable East India Company – one of the earliest Western corporations, formed in 1600 – to the construction of sewerage and water systems. Such corporations were granted the protection of the state and exclusive rights to the proceeds of their endeavours – a government-granted monopoly, similar to intellectual property rights – but only if they stuck to the specified public purpose for which incorporation had been authorized. To be sure, the public benefit of commercial colonial rampages accrued primarily to the West, but there was a core idea that the expeditions were at the pleasure of the sovereign.

Licensing corporations in the early years of the American Republic took on a similar model. It took an act of legislation to charter each corporation and they were again formed for a limited, usually public, purpose – building and running a canal, digging a road, laying railroads or forming a bank – and for a limited term. The idea, at first, was not to enable the deploy-ment of capital generally, but to facilitate the completion of projects for the common good. But the system was cumber-some, with each company requiring a government-granted charter. Free incorporation, without legislative decree, was eventually introduced to open up the possibility of forming a corporation beyond the nepotistic confines of the elite and in order to democratize industry.[3]

As we have seen, the power of the corporation was initially still circumscribed through incorporation laws that restricted the activities and potential scale of industry. Meanwhile, the sense of corporate public responsibility, present from the corporation's beginning, reached a peak in the 1950s with 'managerial capitalism'. The immediate post-war period was a unique time in business. The shared sacrifice of the Second World War produced a socio-economic culture in which it was understood that the post-war prosperity should also be shared. Labour unions were strong and CEOs saw themselves as stewarding vehicles of national wealth creation, with a mostly passive board of directors. The prosperity of corporate America was allowed to radiate out through the economy.

As the Cold War took hold, company managers started to see their role in the ideological struggle as providing evidence that capitalism could provide a better life for workers than communism, through the socialization of the capitalist economy. One commentator wrote in 1960: '[W]hereas 50 or 100 years ago the profit maximizing manager would perhaps have been tolerated in some circles of some communities, today society clearly expects the businessman to act responsibly.'[4] A 1961 *Harvard Business Review* survey of 1,700 executives revealed that approximately 83 per cent of the respondents agreed that: '[F]or corporate executives to act in the interests of shareholders alone, and not also in the interests of employees and consumers, is unethical.'[5]

That was in the early 1960s, ten years before Friedman's diatribe against socially responsible business. But for Friedman and Hayek and the Mont Pelerin gang this logic was back to front: socializing corporations would lead to the stealthy spread of socialism more broadly. When Friedman's article was published in 1970, it was considered far out of the mainstream. But then the 1970s were marked by poor corporate performance, against a backdrop of oil price shocks and stagflation (the unfortunate combination of inflation and unemployment). The passive boards of directors, rubber-stamping the strategies of unconstrained CEOs at the helms of industry, were thought to be part of the problem. High-profile firms were failing and the Watergate scandal came to engulf many public and private firms with revelations of bribes, illegal campaign contributions and dismal corporate governance.

The rise of bureaucracy through the 1950s had been so strong that economist Joseph Schumpeter predicted that it would wipe out the creative force of capitalism, stifling innovation in its drive for predictability and stability. Business executives administering sprawling bureaucracies could easily lose sight of shareholder interests, so there were real concerns about protecting shareholders from managers who were seen to be at best negligent and at worst fraudulent.[6]

As contemporary commentators have tried to unpick the reasons why Friedman's article had such an impact, and how shareholder value eventually took hold, we come back again to the particular context of the 1970s. 'The success of the article was not because the arguments were sound or powerful, but rather because people desperately wanted to believe,'[7] remarks one commentator. The approach was eventually welcomed even by the chastised management, perhaps seeking to reclaim their venerated positions as the captains of industry. Global competition was starting to squeeze profit margins and executives were looking for new, intellectually respectable ideas to boost their revenues. So the suggestion that they could focus totally on making money, and forget about concerns for employees, customers, society or the natural world, was gratefully received. The boost to their own pay packets likely also helped.

## *Of bishops and brothers*

Friedman was not making the idea of shareholder value up in 1970. Shareholder value was tentatively established in US law in 1919 and later embedded, somewhat uneasily, as part of UK law in the 1990s. Nevertheless, shareholder value is actually quite a peculiar sort of rule: it has its origins in law, yes, but equivalent legal principles in other fields of law will have reams of cases affirming and reaffirming the core tenets, shaping the boundaries of the rule and excising the exceptions. For shareholder value there is no well-established body of case law or specific statute – just a few by-the-way musings from judges, and fragmentary decisions. Shareholder value is also more or less unenforceable. In fact, many statutes, including those in many US states and in the UK, provide for the opposite of shareholder value: they permit companies to consider interests beyond those of the shareholders, especially in day-to-day decision making. And yet this is not what many directors do.

To explore the legal origins of shareholder value we must start in a car factory, in Detroit, Michigan. Not just any car factory, but Henry Ford's car factory where, in 1914, Ford declared a corporate policy to invest all capital profits into vertically integrating into iron, hiring more workers, and reducing the cost of his cars for customers 'to spread the benefits of this industrial system to the greatest possible number, to help them build up their lives and their homes'. Ford announced a $10 million bonus fund for workers, and thousands of people lined up outside the factory gates to secure a job. But his fellow shareholders, the Dodge brothers, were not pleased, even though, if Ford's policies had been implemented, they were still due to receive annual income of $120,000 on a $200,000 investment, a rich return of 66 per cent (plus the special dividends of $3.6 million they had already received).

The brothers took Ford to court and their lawyer described Ford's plans, with a touch of hyperbole, as 'a purely reckless, chimerical, hare-brained scheme to spend the money of these stockholders in a plan that will, of its own force, break down and bring ruin and destruction on every man who has any money invested in it'.[8] The court at least partly agreed. Finding against Ford, the Michigan Supreme Court forcefully declared:

> A business corporation is organized and carried on primarily for the profit of the stockholders. The powers of the directors are to be employed for that end. The discretion of directors is to be exercised in the choice of means to attain that end, and does not extend to a change in the end itself, to the reduction of profits, or to the non-distribution of profits among stockholders in order to devote them to other purposes.[9]

The court was clear: the primary responsibility of the directors, and the purpose of a corporation, is to create financial gain for the shareholders. They can choose how to do it, but do it they must.

And so it began. The case has not been relied upon often for its precedential value in US courts since, but the mere existence of the court's pronouncement has had far-reaching consequences for the durability of the shareholder value concept.[10]

The Delaware Court of Chancery affirmed this position when it arose in the course of an attempted hostile takeover by eBay in the early 2000s of personal ads website craigslist, the popular marketplace for second-hand couches, sports memorabilia and dodgy housemates.[11] eBay became a shareholder in craigslist when a previous shareholder became frustrated with craigslist's lack of ambition to monetize and so decided to sell his share to eBay. The founders of craigslist then acted to resist any further takeover by eBay on the grounds that they were trying to protect craigslist's social values and community-centric company culture, which would be threatened by an outright acquisition by the corporate giant. The Delaware Chancery Court, in probably one of the only times that it has ever been on first-name terms with defendants, said: 'Jim and Craig did prove that they personally believe craigslist should not be about the business of stockholder wealth maximization, now or in the future.' Then, here comes the 'but': 'Having chosen a for-profit corporate form, the craigslist directors are bound by the fiduciary duties and standards that accompany that form. Those standards include acting to promote the value of the corporation for the benefit of its stockholders. The "Inc." after the company name has to mean at least that.' If you want to do good, form a charity, they said. For-profit companies exist to make money.

In fact, the main precedent in the UK is actually based in charity law, where the board of directors of a company is mirrored by the board of trustees of a charity. In 1992, the Bishop of Oxford sought a declaration by the court that the trustees investing Church property in order to generate returns to fund the stipends of clergy people should not be investing in ways that conflicted with the Christian faith.[12] In particular, he did not think it right that the trustees should choose to, or feel compelled to, invest in companies with activities in South Africa, whilst apartheid continued to blight that country.

Seventy years and thousands of miles apart, the court's decision resonated with that of the Michigan Supreme Court against Henry Ford. The court held that: 'Most charities need money; and the more of it there is available the more the trustees can seek to accomplish.' In other words, the social impact of a charity is to be achieved through its charitable works only. Any investments it makes with its endowment should seek maximal returns, so that additional income may be deployed towards its charitable aims. The investments themselves, however, should have profit as their focus, not social good. In the corporate world in the UK this is interpreted as the equivalent of maximizing profits and shareholder wealth. Companies should make as much money as possible for their shareholders, who can then contribute to the public good, however they wish, with their freshly minted profits.

This position was problematically cemented into UK law in the mid-2000s as the UK Companies Act was undergoing its once-per-generation update. Many argued vigorously for a 'pluralist' approach, based on the idea that companies should serve a wider range of interests, not subordinate to or as a means of achieving shareholder value, but as valid in their own right. But others argued that maximizing shareholder value is the best means of securing overall prosperity. The efficiency, trickle-down, invisible hand argument won, with one minor concession: in the UK, shareholder value was to become 'enlightened'.

'Enlightened shareholder value' under section 172 of the Companies Act 2006 means that directors owe a duty to 'promote the success of the company for the benefit of its members' (i.e. the shareholders), but here comes the important bit: 'and in doing so *have regard . . . to*' a host of factors listed in the statute: the long-term consequences, the interests of the company's employees, suppliers and customers, the impact of the company's operations on the community and the environment, the company's reputation, and fairness as between the shareholders.[13]

The drafters were clear that in most cases, the 'success' of the company will be defined in economic terms, looking to a long-term increase in shareholder value, but they felt that listing the multitude of factors relevant to this would have a major influence on changing behaviour and the climate of decision making in business. Unfortunately, things have not quite turned out that way.

The bit that seems to really stick in people's minds is the duty to promote the success of the company 'for the benefit of its members'. This conveniently overlooks the long-established legal principle that directors owe their duties primarily not to shareholders but to the company itself. 'Enlightened shareholder value' does allow directors to take into account the interests of stakeholders, but it falls short of truly catalysing business to become a force for good. It is permissive, not compelling: it allows directors to pursue non-financial aims without fear of being sued, but it does not force or even full-throatedly encourage them to do so – at least it has not been interpreted that way. Indeed, the only party with power to enforce the stakeholder protections that the law purports to give are the shareholders.

As elsewhere in corporate law, 'enlightened shareholder value' retains enough ambiguity and lack of enforceability for directors to drive a truck through, and the disregard for stakeholder interests is reinforced through other limbs of corporate regulation like tax law and accounting practices. The law provides ample cover for shareholder value-minded companies, and despite any continued debate amongst legal scholars as to the status in law of shareholder value, wealth maximization is simply what many companies do.

Even the 2014 pronouncement by the Supreme Court in *Hobby Lobby* – a case concerning corporate religious freedoms but which included a declaration by the court that companies are not required to maximize shareholder value, nor have they ever been – cannot shake shareholder value from the corporate psyche: '[M]odern corporate law,' the Supreme Court said, 'does not require for-profit corporations to pursue profit at the expense of everything else.'[14] But when this statement was made, by the highest court in the United States, American businesses did not turn around and change the foundations of how they do business – free, as it turns out they always had been, to do good for society. Instead, nothing changed. Shareholder value lives on.

Shareholder value's unenforceability seems not to undermine its endurance as a governing principle. In fact, no case exists holding a director liable for not maximizing shareholder value in the everyday operations of the company since *Dodge v Ford*.[15] If anything, judges have mostly seen fit to prevent shareholders from enforcing wealth maximization when investors have sued companies for paying their employees too much; for failing to pursue a profit opportunity; for not maximizing a settlement amount in a negotiation; or for failing to lawfully avoid taxes (yes, people bring such claims!).[16] And as long ago as the 1800s, the English courts declared that they would not be called upon to second-guess how managers run businesses. The courts are loath to intervene lest they be required themselves to, in the words of Lord Eldon from a case in 1812, 'take the management of every playhouse and brewhouse in the kingdom'.[17] And yet the principles of profit maximization, of shareholder primacy and the idea that maximizing returns for shareholders is what companies must do, have been fully embraced. It is what the 'Inc.' stands for, after all.

## Shareholder memes

If shareholder value is such a bad idea, with widely accepted costs as a contributor to inequality, industrial concentration and thus higher prices, destruction of the environment, and a whole host of other social ills, why do we not just get rid of it? This, it turns out, is actually three questions: what are the justifications for shareholder value (the 'why?' question), and how does shareholder value in practice endure (the 'what?' and 'how?' questions).

The first justification for shareholder value is that the shareholders own the company, therefore they have the right for it to be run in their interests. This point is easily dispatched: the English courts have made clear that the shareholders are definitively not owners of the company,[18] and we can easily see why, as one commentator puts it: 'ownership [of stock] is literally a betting slip, and it is mere coincidence that the slip relates to a share of stock, rather than a horse or a football game.'[19] Renowned legal scholar Lynn Stout explains further: 'corporations are legal entities that own themselves, just as human entities own themselves'.[20] Shareholders do not own the company, they own shares – and often not for very long. They cannot sell the company; they can only sell their shares.[21]

Another argument is that shareholders put their capital at risk so they therefore deserve to be protected. But many other 'investors' also tie their fate to the company, and they too lack contracts sufficient to protect them – in fact, often they are even more exposed. Leading management academic Colin Mayer argues that contractual rights are extremely restricted for factory workers who may lose their jobs, the workers in Rana Plaza who lost their lives, the citizens of smog-filled cities, the taxpayers who bailed out the banks.[22] And contracts are non-existent for future generations who will inherit a planet in crisis.

Meanwhile, shareholders do not even seem to be investing risk capital any more; they invest in the secondary market, buy and sell at whim, and extract value beyond their investment. Economist William Lazonick has shown that the flow of cash from the stock market to companies is actually negative.[23] Shareholders attempt to harvest value that they played no part in creating, and exit before the true costs are reckoned. Lazonick calls this the 'legalized looting' of the industrial corporation.[24]

These are the legal arguments. The final argument is economic, and it comes back to the invisible hand. On this argument shareholder returns act as a signal to investors, allowing them to shuffle resources around the economy to their most efficient use. If this signal is distorted, or if the control over managers by shareholders is loosened, there will be an inevitable drag on the efficiency of the economy.[25] This assumes quite a bit of knowledge on the part of shareholders, whereas in fact it seems that even gargantuan investors like BlackRock, which has over $6.5 trillion of assets under management, keep themselves bizarrely under-resourced to monitor even the financial performance of its investee companies, let alone their performance on some grander, economy-wide welfare metric.

Perhaps, though, the more interesting question is: why do we have shareholder value, not in theory but in reality, when it is barely respectable law, it is certainly not respectable practice, and it cannot even be enforced? Lynn Stout caused quite a stir in the legal community when she declared that managers of public companies have 'no enforceable legal duty to maximize shareholder value'. She continues:

> Certainly they [directors] can choose to maximize profits; but they can also choose to pursue any other objective that is not unlawful, including taking care of employees and suppliers, pleasing customers, benefiting the community and the broader society, and preserving and protecting the corporate entity itself. Shareholder primacy is a managerial choice – not a legal requirement.[26]

Shareholders do indeed find it very hard to enforce shareholder value in the courts, and yet companies often claim to, or attempt to, maximize shareholder value anyway. It may be a managerial choice, but it is a choice that company managers make repeatedly. Prioritizing shareholders is not a legal obligation – but tell that to your lawyer and they will likely look at you as if you have become a flat-Earther.

The pressure managers and investors feel to conform to the shareholder value norm is very real, even for those who have tried, along the way, to do some good. Consider the forces that drove Ben & Jerry's to sell to global conglomerate Unilever.[27] Ben & Jerry's was a pioneering, socially minded company before that concept had entered the popular consciousness. Founders Ben Cohen and Jerry Greenfield pursued a double bottom line of social good and financial return (they referred to this as the 'double-dip') by committing 7.5 per cent of their profits to a charitable foundation; by buying ingredients from suppliers who employed disadvantaged populations and supported the local economy; by initially raising money through a local public offering to Vermont residents; by being one of the first companies to offer health care benefits to employees' same sex partners; by using eco materials in its packaging; and by registering voters in-store in the run-up to elections. Their ambitions were grand, and why not? For its Chocolate Fudge Brownie ice cream, the company purchased the brownies from Greyston Bakery, a producer employing formerly homeless, low-income and disenfranchised people, about which Ben & Jerry's said: 'It's no stretch to say that when you eat our Chocolate Fudge Brownie ice cream, you're striking a blow for economic and social justice.' It was a lofty, admirable and delightfully preposterous goal to combat social injustice with ice cream.

But when it came down to it, as a publicly traded company they felt under pressure to sell – or, some would say, sell out – to Unilever, in 2000, considering the litigation risk of resisting the takeover to be too great. Indeed, three class action lawsuits alleging that the directors were breaching their fiduciary duties to shareholders by failing to maximize shareholder value were filed whilst the deal was still being negotiated.[28] Jerry Greenfield said subsequently that they did not want to sell the business but felt that their legal duties to shareholders ran counter to their hearts and ultimately superseded their sentiments about the company.

So shareholder value exists in law but only weakly. It is unenforceable, but company directors believe they have to do it anyway. Can a simple belief, then, be self-perpetuating? In the 1970s, evolutionary biologist Richard Dawkins developed the concept of 'selfish genes'.[29] The idea was that we think that we fall in love, have children and form communities through free will, but actually we are just hosts for our selfish genes, hell-bent on their own propagation. The internet generation of today may be surprised to learn that the origin of the word 'meme' was Dawkins' generalization of this theory to the cultural spread of things like language, religion, melodies, ideas, fashions and schools of thought. Coining a new word, he helpfully included a guide to pronunciation, stipulating that it should rhyme with 'cream'.

It is useful to think of money as a meme – an idea that has been extremely successful at replicating itself in the minds of human beings. The corporation and shareholder value are the two companion fictions that facilitate the reproduction of money. We think that money exists because it is useful to us, as a means of exchange – the more useful it is, the more money we make. But what if the runaway success of money, and its ability to grow seemingly exponentially, owes its cause not to the utility of money to us but to the reverse: because we, and our human economic interactions and legal structures, are useful to it?

Money finds a way to ensure the continuance and spread of shareholder value despite its shaky legal standing. Money, of course, has no will of its own, rather it is like water, following the path of least resistance, flowing into the available cracks and spaces, eroding the institutions through which it courses, adopting its own path and suffusing the system with its presence like a high water table in a porous aquifer. If we let it, money will stop us from acting to control the corporate power and corporate abuse that fuels its growth – it has no reason to step out of the way.

Perhaps precisely because the law and logic serve to undermine the concept of shareholder value, the mechanisms the market finds for enforcing it are myriad: the threat of hostile takeovers if management performance lags, through the 'market for corporate control' facilitated by robust capital markets and the watchful eyes of scores of securities analysts; institutional investors in public companies, enjoying special privileges of access to management due to their greater stockholding, with the opportunity to remind managers who controls their appointment; strong shareholder wealth maximization norms, established through socialization in business schools and on the job, and through the constant utterance of the firm's lawyers. And of course some directors are also shareholders, and vice versa – a very effective mechanism for aligning shareholder and managerial interests.

Shareholder value is an idea, a very powerful idea. Legal scholars divert themselves with tireless debates as to whether shareholder value really exists in theory, even though it plainly does in practice. Whether or not shareholder wealth maximization is written into law, people seem to think that it is. We need to accept this and think about how we can begin to challenge such a powerful norm. As it stands, the idea of shareholder value has seeped into our core understanding of how business works, and the abdication of corporate responsibility that it mandates leads to a proliferation of destructive corporate power.

## Tug of war

On the face of it, we seem to have a system in conflict: antitrust argues for maximum 'consumer welfare' and profit minimization whereas shareholder value demands the opposite – profit maximization at any cost.[30]

But what at first seems to be a system pulling in two directions turns out to be a mechanism oriented towards a single goal: shareholder wealth. The norm of shareholder value is much stronger than the law of consumer welfare – for the simple reason that consumer welfare under Borkian antitrust is actually corporate welfare, since whatever is good for the presumptively efficient company is assumed to be good for the consumer too. Competition law has typically ignored what happens inside companies, which is where shareholder value casts its spell, focusing instead on dynamics in the market. It is therefore assumed that companies act in a certain way – a way that, when constrained by competition from rival firms, benefits everyone. Antitrust therefore did not need to concern itself with the internal workings of the company, as the market would see to it that consumers would get the lowest prices.

The meme of money propagates itself in the cocoon of the shareholder value company and spreads its wings by hunting for other forms of power. Shareholder value pushes the company to exploit market failures, including by annexing market power and producing externalities, and antitrust does little to stop it. And with money amassing power, other regulators will struggle to prevent the transmission of the spillovers of this industriousness on to society.

The whole of the corporate world, in the US and UK at least, is designed around shareholders, including the defence of the monopolistic companies they invest in. There is no real corporate responsibility. We seem to have forgotten that the formation of a corporation was, and still is, a publicly granted privilege allowed only at the sufferance of the state. Corporate law no longer controls power – as it did before incorporation laws were watered down – and it no longer enforces responsibility either.

As Chief Justice Strine of Delaware, the most important American court for companies, given that the majority of Fortune 500 companies are organized under Delaware corporate law, explains:

> Under the current legal rules and power structures within corporate law, it is naïve to expect that corporations will not externalize costs when they can. It is naïve to think that they will treat workers the way we would want to be treated. It is naïve to think that corporations will not be tempted to sacrifice long-term value maximizing investments when powerful institutional investors prefer short-term corporate finance gimmicks.

It is naïve to think that, over time, corporations will not tend to push against the boundaries of whatever limits the law sets, when mobilized capital focused on short-term returns is the only constituency with real power over who manages the corporations. And it is naïve to think that institutional investors themselves will behave differently if action is not taken to address the incentives that cause their interests to diverge from those people whose funds they invest.[31]

Of course the motivations of the company matter, he says, and affect how it goes about competing, and the lengths to which it will go to secure a profit. But the neoliberal economic paradigm of free markets and freedom for the powerful calls upon our willing naivety, over and over – and, blindly, we give it.

Some have referred to antitrust as a religion,[32] and to those in the neoliberal sect as a 'disciplined army of the faithful',[33] and it is true that, in the past, a lot was taken on faith. My career crisis as a disillusioned competition lawyer, and my frustration with the limits of what can be achieved with competitive markets, pushed me to dig deeper and lift the lid on the company to see whether *how* companies are run could explain *why* markets do not always generate good results for people. Making fizzy drinks markets competitive and the products as cheap as possible seemed to be entirely beside the point; I could not be blindly faithful any more.

We cannot expect better corporate conduct whilst the myth of the shareholder value duty persists. The biggest and most powerful firms, in particular, should have a clear responsibility to respect the public interest in a manner befitting the immense privileges bestowed on the corporate form as a money-making machine.

Shareholder value is not the law – or it does not have to be, if we collectively agree that it is not. But doing so involves letting go of one more free market myth first.

**SUMMARY**

**Myth #5:** The law requires companies to maximize financial value for shareholders.

**Reality:** The law is being wilfully misinterpreted to our collective detriment as it does not require companies to maximize shareholder profit.

# 6.

# *A nation of shareholders*

Myth #6: We are all shareholders; we all benefit from corporate
focus on shareholders' interests

Whenever I think about the nature of the corporate entity, I am
reminded of John Steinbeck's novel *The Grapes of Wrath*. Set during the Great Depression, the book is a powerful indictment of
the insatiable greed of the capitalist system. When a poor family
of tenant farmers is kicked off the land their ancestors settled,
they plead with their landlord for a reprieve. He responds:

'The bank – the monster has to have profits all the time. It can't
wait. It'll die . . . When the monster stops growing, it dies. It
can't stay one size.'

So the tenants are forced to move off the land because the
landlords need to pay the bank. The dialogue continues as the
owners say:

'We're sorry. It's not us. It's the monster. The bank isn't like a
man.'
  'Yes, but the bank is only made of men.'
  'No, you're wrong there – quite wrong there. The bank is
something else than men. It happens that every man in a bank
hates what the bank does, and yet the bank does it. The bank is

something more than men, I tell you. It's the monster. Men made it, but they can't control it.'

Later, when the hired farm hands come to run the tenants off the land, the tenants want revenge; they don't want to go without a fight. One demands:

'But where does it stop? Who can we shoot? I don't aim to starve to death before I kill the man that's starving me.'

The response comes:

'I don't know. Maybe there's nobody to shoot. Maybe the thing isn't men at all . . .'

A company is a figment of our collective imagination; if you poke it then it disappears. A fictional organization can have only fictional responsibilities. 'Men made it, but they can't control it.' But like in *The Wizard of Oz*, there is actually someone standing behind the spectre. A few very powerful someones. They did not create the system – they did not create the monster – but, nevertheless, there they stand, baiting the monster to do their bidding.

## *Behind every powerful company is a powerful man*

Shareholder value might be much less problematic if we were all shareholders – but, alas, we are not. In theory, the pursuit of profits benefits us all indirectly through the spread of efficiency throughout the economy, trickling down to make everyone better off, but in practice the efficiencies are distributed unevenly, turning the corporation into a chute through which profits are propelled towards the already wealthy.

In the 1980s, Margaret Thatcher set out her vision for how Britain was to become a 'nation of shareholders', where owning shares would be as common as owning a car. The idea was to spread economic independence, and also to get the public invested, both literally and metaphorically, in the well-being of business. 'Popular capitalism' was advocated in terms of empowerment: 'power through ownership to the man and woman in the street, given confidently with an open hand'.[1]

Sounds like a great idea, but did it actually happen? If we are all shareholders then we do not have to hope that rapacious companies will benefit us indirectly through innovation and cheap goods and consumer welfare, we stand to get a direct payout. But there is a question here that is begged but so very rarely asked: who actually are these shareholders for whom the corporate sector is run?

The answer is: we mostly do not know who owns the companies we buy from, work for, transact with, subsidize and bail out. Part of the difficulty is that the sources of information are patchy or hard to access, but also many shares are held in nominee accounts that shield the identity of the true owner – for legitimate and sometimes illegitimate reasons – and shares are often legally owned by an asset manager on behalf of a pension fund, for example, but the identity of the ultimate beneficiary will be undisclosed. The situation is even more murky with privately held companies, although countries are increasingly requiring private companies to disclose significant beneficial owners, as part of the global crackdown against corruption and money laundering.

What we do know is that whilst governments today still celebrate whenever the stock markets reach new highs, and lament when they reach new lows, everyday people are not sharing directly in these booms and busts. In the US, the top 10 per cent of American households own 84 per cent of all stocks, with half of that owned by the top 1 per cent, whilst the bottom

80 per cent own only 7 per cent.[2] So we have most of the people owning not very much of the so-called public markets. Although almost half of households own some shares, the value is heavily skewed towards the rich, with 94 per cent of the very rich having more than $10,000 in shares, and only 27 per cent of the middle class having the same.[3] Meanwhile, the middle class is laden with debt, and although the global economy has recovered from the financial crisis, the wealth of the middle class has not bounced back fully, relative to the recovery of the wealthy. In the UK, the most recent surveys show that around 20 per cent of households hold shares, but the vast majority hold only a few and they are not regularly traded.[4] And we do not have data on the value spread of those shares across wealth brackets. As for the rest of the world, over half a billion people own shares worldwide.[5] But again, there is almost nothing known about who holds these shares, what they are worth, and how wealthy these shareholders are already.

Meanwhile, some shareholders are able to treat the companies they control as their own personal ATMs, even if real jobs are at stake. It is usually only in extreme circumstances that we push aside the fiction of the company and look at the founders and owners behind the corporate mirage. With the collapse of British retailer BHS in 2017, which resulted in the loss of 11,000 jobs and left a shortfall in the employee pension scheme of £571 million, eyes finally turned to billionaire Philip Green. Investors, including Green, had pocketed £586 million from a deal selling the company to a serial bankrupt, precipitating the implosion of a British high street institution. Green agreed to pay £363 million out of what he considered to be his own money, but he found the questions raised about his levels of wealth irksome. His comments reflect the extent to which many business people have internalized the idea that their wealth is completely deserved: 'I feel like I've got to justify I had the ability to pay, that my family has got a yacht, that I'm living a nice lifestyle. Thank goodness, along my journey, I was very successful and therefore I was able to pay.'[6] In Green's eyes the former employees and pensioners should be glad that Green had enough money to partially bail them out – even if from a disaster of his own making.

MPs, on the other hand, leading an inquiry into the collapse of BHS, found that Green had 'systematically extracted hundreds of millions of pounds from BHS, paying very little tax and fantastically enriching himself and his family, leaving the company and its pension fund weakened to the point of the inevitable collapse of both.'[7] And yet total extraction of corporate value by shareholders is what shareholder value can mean, when taken to its logical conclusion. The scandal was a reminder that the norms of protecting the shareholder over and above any other constituency are well embedded with the heads of company executives, shareholders and their legal advisers.

Shareholder value does not serve us all as shareholders in equal measure. It turns out that the 'nation of shareholders' argument is a little like saying that anyone who has ever bought a lottery ticket has some stake in this week's winnings, even if only a few people ever hit the jackpot and your ticket may no longer even be valid. It is not a compelling reason to engineer a whole economy around the needs of the winners on the basis that we are all 'in it to win it'.

And yet any attempt to weaken the grip of shareholder value faces the argument that maximizing returns for shareholders is a necessary evil for the future pensioners who will rely upon stocks for their income.[8] But these pensioners-to-be also rely on safe and well-paid jobs whilst they are working and clean, breathable air whilst they raise their families and when they retire, so it is very selective thinking to zoom in only on their financial needs as shareholders.

The campaigning charity ShareAction argues that since the public is invested in publicly listed companies via its pensions, we should have a greater say over how those companies are run, and they should be operated for the public benefit.[9] It is true that pension pots can be large – \$2 trillion in the UK, \$300 billion for two pension plans in Canada, \$500 billion for two plans in the Netherlands, \$300 billion for a pension plan for public workers in California – with global pension assets being worth \$41 trillion.[10] But that actually under-represents the many ways in which the public and the state invest in these companies, from providing the use of public infrastructure to educating and ensuring the health of their employees. If we think about the investment chain, with shareholders at the top and workers and consumers at the bottom – we live and work in the real economy at the bottom of the chain, but shareholder value and monopoly draw money and resources up, slurping it up through the company as if through a straw, to the top, where participation is much more uneven. We absolutely should have a say over how our investee companies are run, and our influence should reflect the full extent of our investment, not just our shareholdings.

## Money maketh the man

For executives, the reframing of corporate responsibility to prioritize taking care of shareholders only has proven highly remunerative. As MIT Professor Thomas Kochan puts it:

> An entire generation of managers and executives has been indoctrinated with the view that their primary, if not sole, responsibility is to attend to shareholder interests and, even worse, attend to and shape their own compensation and rewards to be aligned with short-term shareholder value.[11]

In the 1980s, a typical top chief executive in the UK was paid approximately 20 times as much as the average British worker.[12] By 2002 this had risen to 70 times the average salary, and by 2014 to almost 150 times. Across the FTSE 100, between 2010 and 2015, the average pay of company directors increased by 47 per cent, whilst average employee pay rose by just 7 per cent. This whilst Oxfam has reported that it takes just four days for a CEO from one of the top five global fashion brands to earn what a Bangladeshi garment worker, like those killed in the tragic Rana Plaza factory collapse, will earn in an entire lifetime.[13]

Executives can 'shape their compensation' by having their preferred packages rubber-stamped by others in their elite group. But if their pay is linked to the share price – justified by a desire to better align managers' interests with those of shareholders – they can directly manipulate the share price through buybacks. A share buyback occurs when, instead of investing in a company's productive capacity, directors arrange to buy back shares off the investors, to return cash to the shareholders (often including themselves) but also to boost the share price by artificially increasing demand for the shares. There are various circumstances in which returning money to shareholders in this way might be sensible but when whole industries are raiding the corporate coffers to deliver returns to shareholders, at the expense of pretty much every other stakeholder, it would seem to be a sign that something is amiss. Economist William Lazonick shows that the total remuneration of the 500 highest paid executives in the US averaged $24.4 million in 2013.[14] Of this, the gains from exercising stock options and the vesting of stock awards amounted to 84 per cent in 2013, with the combination of salaries and bonuses only accounting for 5 per cent of executive pay in 2013. Lazonick has referred to this financialization of the corporation as a 'socioeconomic disease'. In 2018, share buybacks reached a value of $1 trillion.

The irony is that in trying to align managers with their own interests, shareholders have created a beast that they cannot tame. As one *Harvard Business Review* article puts it:

> One could spin this as a tale of wily, self-interested managers' taking advantage of investors – because it is. But it's also a case of shareholders' pushing for change and then proving incapable of controlling it. The adversarial, stock-market-oriented approach to pay appears to have motivated executives to think more like mercenaries and less like stewards.[15]

Men made it, but they cannot control it.

## *'Minority' shareholders*

If the image you have in your mind of a generic shareholder is of a white man then, in the US and Europe, you may not be far off. In terms of gender inequality, although there has been very little research into the phenomenon, we can expect that women will be under-represented in the 'shareholder class'. According to Gallup, there is only a small gap in the percentage of share ownership between men and women in the US, with 56 per cent of men owning shares against 52 per cent of women.[16] But this tells us nothing of the relative value of the shareholdings – it may be that 52 per cent of women have bought a lottery ticket but they may not be making substantial winnings.

Most 'everyday shareholders' own their shares via a pension scheme, and the size of the individual pension pots are closely tied to lifetime earnings. But the median woman in 2017 in America held just $42,000 in retirement savings compared to $123,000 for men.[17] The situation is even more dire for transgender people. Transgender Americans experience poverty at double the rate of the general population, and transgender people of colour experience even higher rates.[18]

Men control over 80 per cent of corporations, and women make up only 6 per cent of CEOs in Fortune 500 companies.[19] Over the last few decades, women have increased their participation in the economy as workers and consumers in their own right. But the private companies they work for and buy from – whose questionable conduct they suffer the burden of, along with the general populace – are run on behalf of a wealthy elite comprised mostly of men. This is profoundly unjust, and it is not a sustainable way to run capitalism.

There has been very little research into the racial divide in stock ownership[20] but the overall trend seems to be as you might expect. In the US, black and Latin households hold much less stock than white; 60 per cent of white households have retirement accounts and/or own some stock, but only 34 per cent of black households and 30 per cent of Latin households do.[21] As with the middle class, minorities have tended to hold their wealth in their homes, not through stocks, in part because they have less wealth to invest. Meanwhile, poor, minority households are disproportionately affected by imbalances of power in the workplace, they are reliant on precarious and poorly paid jobs, and they are exploited in consumer markets where companies take advantage of uninformed purchasing decisions or consumer biases.

We generally shy away from the kinds of language used by Marxists – who decried the exploitation of one class by another – but the uncomfortable reality is that our corporate system, which extracts value from consumers, workers and the planet, and delivers to shareholders, is one in which a white, wealthy elite of men profits at the expense of the poor – brown, black, Latin and Asian men and women and transgendered people, and every other 'minority' that exists.

## *People-powered companies*

Shareholder value was meant to be a mechanism for holding corporate managers to account but has instead served to weaponize the firm into a tool for inequality and power – turning every company into a prospective robber baron.[22]

We rely on a collective mythology that successful companies deserve their higher profits and rich people deserve their wealth, for both have made some noble sacrifice or have shared their talents with the world. Another myth is that money and power can be dissipated through taxation, redistribution and regulation, but instead it compounds and accumulates whilst wealth is removed from the real economy altogether. And finally, there comes another myth: that the rich – those benefiting from these higher profits and higher returns – are all of us, all of our savings and all of our pensions. But we are not all shareholders, not to the same extent.

Since we are not all shareholders, we can let go, finally, of the idea that shareholder value benefits the general public. We benefit neither indirectly from the efficiency of markets nor directly as investors – or not enough to compensate for the harms perpetuated in the name of shareholder value and competition. Democratizing the firm – real democratization, not just empowerment of shareholders – would allow the public to share in the creativity of capitalism and to direct companies away from the most egregious public harms. We have our work cut out for us.

---

**SUMMARY**

**Myth #6:** We are all shareholders; we all benefit from corporate focus on shareholders' interests.

**Reality:** Most shareholders are already wealthy.

---

## PART TWO

# How to make corporate capitalism work for people and planet

# 7

# Stakeholder antitrust

We have now dismantled the six myths of free market competition, which means we are ready to face reality.

**Myth #1:** Free markets are competitive.

**Reality:** Free market competition creates power. In fact, 'competition' has come to be synonymous with domination and corporate power.

**Myth #2:** Companies compete by trying to best respond to the needs of society.

**Reality:** Companies compete for power, for the benefit of their shareholders, in ways that harm society.

**Myth #3:** Corporate power is benign.

**Reality:** There are many types of corporate power that allow the powerful to choose how to shape the economy and society in their interests.

**Myth #4:** We already control corporate power with antitrust.

**Reality:** Modern antitrust condones corporate power.

**Myth #5:** The law requires companies to maximize financial value for shareholders.

**Reality:** The law is being wilfully misinterpreted to our collective detriment as it does not require companies to maximize shareholder profit.

**Myth #6:** We are all shareholders; we all benefit from corporate focus on shareholders' interests.

**Reality:** Most shareholders are already wealthy.

With these realities in hand, the primordial blind spot of free market competition can be seen more clearly: competition is a race to power, and companies compete in part by producing social and environmental spillovers they do not have to pay for. Our models of competition minimize or ignore these aspects of competition, and it is on this basis that the antitrust regime does not, after all is said and done, produce markets that could genuinely be called 'competitive' or 'efficient'. Markets are instead highly concentrated and replete with social and environmental harms. Competition by itself will not spread power and make everyone better off; instead, we must actively contain any power that arises from market distortions and share out the residual corporate power that we cannot contain to stakeholders so that they may be empowered to protect their own interests.

But these realities do not yet take up the same space that the myths, with their decades of augmentation, have come to occupy – they need their own accompanying narrative and logic to bind them to the structure of twenty-first-century capitalism.

Corporate capitalism currently operates completely untethered from the state that supports it, almost in an attempt to be as much the opposite of command and control, state-governed socialism as possible. But it turns out that, in order to have the best of both worlds – the progress and industry of capitalism, and the socialization of competition and markets – we can take a middle ground. Private corporations can remain in private hands, guided not by the central arm of the state but by the decentralized will of stakeholders embedded within companies.

The aim is to attempt to reap the benefits of fruitful competition by aligning companies to the public interest whilst avoiding the entropic inequality, injustice and negative spillovers that otherwise suffuse and overwhelm the economic system. The free-flowing flood of money and power could be replaced with a controlled irrigation system, directing the creative ability of capitalism towards the cultivation of desired and desirable projects and enterprises.

This can be achieved through a structural change in corporate capitalism, designed to dissipate power through a much more broadly conceived system of antitrust, striking at both the heart and periphery of corporate power. Whatever power cannot be dispersed should be shared, through participatory mechanisms empowering people to engage actively in the stewarding of the markets.

In Part Two of this book, I will present an agenda for this new regime: 'stakeholder antitrust'. Stakeholder antitrust comprises two elements.

1. More robust and democratized antitrust enforcement that works constantly to contain the power that accumulates in free markets
2. A fundamental change in the nature of incorporation and responsibility for the most powerful companies, democratizing these firms and making them directly accountable to stakeholders

Together, these elements will help to ensure that competition really does work in the interests of the public.

## *Power and responsibility*

There are two separate conversations taking place amongst those looking to reform capitalism: on the one hand, some are calling for greater antitrust enforcement to tackle monopoly power and increase competition, and on the other hand, some are looking to soften the harshness of competition by promoting corporate social responsibility. What has not been fully appreciated is that these cannot be two separate policy streams. Market power, left unchecked, will undermine responsibility. Creating more competition will only lead to more spillovers – and the accumulation of power, yet again – if we do not change how firms operate in the economy.

Neither corporate governance, which deals in the responsibilities of companies, nor antitrust, which deals in power, have been adequately serving the public interest – in large part due to a failure to connect the two. Responsibility for all to make money has not served the public interest. Power to the powerful has not served the public interest.

Corporate power was originally controlled through corporate law, which set out the permissible scope of action and mandated responsibility for companies as a condition of their existence – the penalty for going beyond permitted action or for abdicating responsibility was the dissolution of the company. In the past, whenever antitrust was deemed inadequate to contain corporate power, there were proposals to use corporate law to restrain large and powerful companies by removing their limited liability, or by requiring some companies to obtain a specific charter from the government, thereby putting them under the supervision of the state.[1]

Even some in the Chicago School, generally opposed to incursions on corporate freedom, have supported such measures. Henry Simons, one of the School's founders and a Mark I Chicagoan, at one point suggested that all corporations should have the amount of property they own limited, to ensure that no single corporation dominates an industry.[2] But even Mark II Chicagoan Aaron Director, Friedman's brother-in-law and Robert Bork's inspiration, similarly called for an end to the 'unlimited power of corporations', not through antitrust, of which he was deeply suspicious, but through corporate law, by limiting the size of corporations, circumscribing the scope of corporate activities, and more.[3]

It may seem odd that Chicagoans wanted to go further than Sherman Act antitrust to limit corporate activities but actually it was the opposite. Using corporate law as antitrust is like flicking an on and off switch – either the company complies with the restrictions of its corporate charter or it will be dissolved. By contrast, with its granular assessment of economic harm and price effects, modern antitrust could be seen as actually requiring *more* intervention in markets – the arbitrary governmental meddling that Bork derided as useless and damaging.

Relatively few scholars have made the connection between antitrust and corporate governance, despite the origins of antitrust in corporate law.[4] What goes on inside the firm is thought to have no bearing on what happens out on the market.

But given the mutually reinforcing nature of shareholder value and monopoly power, it seems we have missed an opportunity to tackle corporate power at home, on its own turf – inside the company – and to surface responsibility not just towards shareholders but to all those affected by the company's activities. Power and responsibility should be reunited, through corporate law and antitrust, otherwise any siloed attempts to mitigate ruthless competition or dissipate corporate power will fail. This is the core principle of stakeholder antitrust and the basis of a new vision for regulating corporate power in free markets by recognizing, finally, the blind spot of capitalism: that free market competition, unrestrained, allows for the accumulation of power and the transmission of harm.

## *A new vision for antitrust in the twenty-first century*

For a comprehensive response to corporate power we must draw from both the competition and corporate governance spheres, creating a new framework for the control of corporate power – stakeholder antitrust – comprised of both competition and corporate law regulation.

The primary role of the competition regulators will be to enforce, with a renewed seriousness, a reinvigorated antitrust regime that tackles corporate power, broadly construed, head on. Beyond conventional market power over price, regulators will target economic and political power, and the mechanisms that allow companies to leverage the one into the other.

Corporate law will be used to remove the hypnotic hold of shareholder value from the biggest, most powerful and most systemically important companies, in three areas:

1. giving companies broad societal responsibilities, owed by the directors, to balance the privilege of incorporation;
2. creating an infrastructure for stakeholder participation and control over company decision making; and
3. allowing for the regulation of corporate power per se through the threat of dissolution as a last resort.

The idea is not to return to pre-twentieth-century chartering for every company: only the most powerful companies will get this treatment. The regulatory scheme can also be updated in other ways. Instead of using corporate law as a crude tool to snuff out power, greater nuance will be admitted into the analysis by creating a symbiotic relationship between the competition regulator and a new corporations regulator: the competition regulator can identify the most problematic companies and markets, referring them to the corporate regulator for remedy, whilst the corporate regulator pinpoints excess power that can be dissipated through competition or through stakeholder participation. We can draw on over a century of experience in assessing competitive tactics to refine our response to corporate power, conscious always of the inbuilt biases of previous scholarship. The nineteenth-century corporate charters will also be updated to reflect the modern realities of globalization and dispersed shareholdings plus the modern concerns of climate breakdown and social justice.

Power, everywhere, must not be left to accumulate and mature, otherwise only the powerful will be free.

# 8.

## *Speaking truth to market power*

History has presented us with an opportunity: corporate power is in the ascendency but so too is dissatisfaction with the settlement of corporate capitalism and the inequality of wealth and power that characterizes it. Antitrust is high on the agenda for the 2020 US presidential candidates, the European Commission is building up a strong track record of challenging the tech giants, and in 2018/2019 the Federal Trade Commission held a series of hearings on 'Competition and Consumer Protection in the 21st Century', emulating the hearings held by my former professor at Georgetown, the late Robert Pitofsky, when he was FTC Chairman in 1995. Around the world, competition agencies are confronting how to adapt to changing markets, including in the digital space.

But at this moment of reflection, and possible inflection, it is natural that some are resisting the change.[1] Conservative scholars argue that the best way for antitrust to serve the public interest is to interfere with free markets as little as possible and to leave the markets to correct themselves. And just like that, we are back to the invisible hand: we should not try to protect workers and suppliers and small independent businesses by actually protecting them. We should trust that, somehow, their interests will be best served by competition, indirectly. Like the gorgon Medusa or a solar eclipse: whatever you do, do not look directly at it.

Antitrust currently does not significantly engage with the concepts of rent, power and externalities. We look at the potential direction in which prices might move – down is good, up is bad – but base this all on assumptions: small firms cooperating with other small firms are assumed to generate harm with no cost savings; big, vertically integrated firms are assumed to generate efficiencies that can be shared with consumers – whether or not they actually are. But focusing solely on the direction of the price avoids talking about the fairness of the price in the first place – whether it reflects any externalities (usually it does not), whether it is excessive, what it shows about the relative power of the parties involved in the transaction – and avoids completely a discussion of the redistribution of rents within transactions and across society.

But it is nonsensical that a framework centred around 'welfare' continues to ignore the harms to consumers, society and the planet. Antitrust has real world impacts – the reshaping of the industrial and financial world, with the regulatory stamp of approval, for one – and has the potential to impact a whole range of issues, including inequality, resource security, sustainability, climate change, productivity, wages, democracy, globalization, worker exploitation and the future of local economies. It is absurd to say that there is no room in the analytical framework to take account of these issues when the impacts of mergers, cooperation (or lack of cooperation) and monopoly materialize anyway, and the concomitant accumulation of power and money affects our ability to address them separately in 'other regulation'.[2] Any one of these issues could be incorporated into the definition of anti-competitive harms if we wanted them to be, it is a question of degree and implementation.[3] Antitrust may not be the single most proximate factor in relation to these concerns but it is part of the problem, and therefore can be part of the solution. And if antitrust has nothing to say then it will fast recede into irrelevance, replaced by other policies, like industrial policy, which should rightly be its complements.

## *Fighting power with power*

If we want to impose responsibility on the most powerful, to focus on the biggest companies with the biggest impacts, to start where it really matters, where large pots of money and swathes of resources are currently being diverted to promote the extraction of wealth for the already wealthy and the mass transmission of costs on to society, then power must sit at the heart of our inquiry. Corporate power need not be taken as a fact of life. We can consider afresh the morality, justice, influence, esteem, fitness, capability, competence and agreeability of corporate power in its essence.

Antitrust's obsession with price means that everything that is not priced – including externalities – currently does not count; whether the positive externalities of sustainability, cooperation and economic democracy, or the negative externalities of pollution and the strain on the social fabric. Even under the consumer welfare standard it is bizarre that we take account of efficiencies that may accrue to consumers, but not externalities – which may even affect the same consumers. As a first step, we can include these other factors – generally labelled diminishingly as 'non-economic' or 'public interest' concerns – into our analysis of how markets work. Really, why would we not?

And indeed, the law in Europe actually already requires – not just allows but positively requires – consideration of many issues beyond price, including sustainable development, protection and improvement of the environment, social exclusion, social justice, equality, social cohesion, rights of the child, cultural heritage, maintaining high levels of employment, education and human health, as well as technical or economic progress.[4] It is a testament to the effectiveness of the Chicago Jedi mind trick that the European neoliberal import of the 'more economic approach' has thus far prevailed over the actual text of the EU Treaties.

Externalities can be used as an indicator of power, and vice versa. If a company has market power, there may be externalities that it is able to emit. If we see an industry with large externalities, we may look for sources of power that allow the companies in that industry to continue functioning without a reckoning. The production of externalities itself constitutes a method of unfair competition.[5] Saving costs or generating 'efficiencies' by using 'free' natural resources is, in effect, a way of cheating the economic system. Just as prices can be excessive, so too can social costs. On this view, the preservation of the natural commons – our shared environmental and social resources – should become a legal responsibility of all companies throughout corporate regulation. Within antitrust we currently look at the efficiency of resource exploitation when we could instead be looking at the efficiency of resource preservation.

The biggest change to competition analysis under stakeholder antitrust would be that efficiencies or cost savings, in theory beneficial to consumers, would not necessarily 'compensate' for harms to other stakeholders. And we might also accept that not all benefits and harms can be reduced to monetary measures. Prices would remain relevant, not primarily as an indicator of harm to consumers but instead as a gauge of power – the transfer of rents from consumers to producers would be part of the analysis of power.

The stakeholder antitrust that I am arguing for would maintain a healthy scepticism towards the efficiency of big business and an open-mindedness towards pro-social cooperation. Vertical restraints and actions by dominant companies would be scrutinized more closely for potential exclusion or exploitation of competitors and customers, and a broader range of factors would be considered in relation to both horizontal and vertical mergers.[6] The entire basis for accepting efficiencies as a justification for corporate conduct would be taken in the context of shareholder value and the tendency of firms operating within that paradigm to funnel profits and cost savings towards shareholders, not consumers or society at large.

There is also a need to level the playing field between the regulator and the regulated. In part, this will be achieved through a reinvigoration of antitrust and any deconcentrating effect this has on industry. But in the meantime, the regulators should be given greater powers of investigation, in recognition of the stark information asymmetry that exists between companies and competition authorities. In the UK, Lord Tyrie, the Chairman of the Competition and Markets Authority, called for just such amendments to UK practice in 2019, including greater powers to impose fines, greater access to evidence, and the power to take action to halt potentially harmful conduct before the full resolution of the case.[7]

## Identifying power

Concurrently with dispersing excess power through reinvigorated enforcement, competition regulators would have a central role in identifying corporate power and prescribing the appropriate response. Stakeholder antitrust would seek to identify power in the broadest sense: market, economic and political power, including the power to inflict social harm. Competition authorities would consider whether conduct by competitors, or frictions in the market, facilitate the accumulation of power or the production of externalities. Even if prevailing market prices are low, there may be grounds for intervention based on the power to extract rents through externalities or the power to avoid or distort regulation – we must remind ourselves that the prices may be low for an objectionable reason.

Under stakeholder antitrust, the competition authority's infrared goggles would be switched back from 'price' mode to 'power'. Identification of power involves interrogating whether a party has economic power over the conditions of the market – not just price but quality, the path of innovation, industry standards and the architecture of the market – and/or political power to influence how the market is regulated, the regulation of other market actors, the direction of policymaking, the flows of information and the shaping of market truths.

We have ignored power for so long that we are somewhat ill equipped to identify it with precision within antitrust, although Zephyr Teachout and Lina Khan's taxonomy of power is a useful start.[8] The 2018 European Commission guidelines on Significant Market Power in regulated digital markets take an expansive view of the indicia of power – requiring national competition authorities to consider, amongst other things:

- barriers to entry
- barriers to expansion
- absolute and relative size of the company
- any control of infrastructure not easily duplicated
- technological and commercial advantages or superiority
- absence of or low countervailing buying power
- easy or privileged access to capital markets/financial resources
- economies of scale
- network effects
- vertical integration, and
- absence of potential competition.[9]

These guidelines could act as an initial blueprint for the analysis of market power, and could be applied, with some tweaking, to economic and political power.

## *Democratizing antitrust*

Once power is detected, the policy responses will flow from the following questions.

- Who has power?
- How can that power be counterbalanced?
- Should the powerful be given more responsibility?
- Can that power be shared with the powerless within the structure of the company or the market?

To ensure that the public interest is served by this new, emboldened antitrust, and not merely folded into another technocratic exercise, we must make allowance not just for the inclusion of public interest factors in the technical analysis of power but for the democratization of the process of competition law enforcement as well. With the current focus on price, and an assumption that the welfare of consumers and society could be reduced to that metric, there has been little desire to make the process of investigations more inclusive. That is beginning to change. Nobel-winning economist Jean Tirole, who won the prize in 2014 for his work on market power and regulation, has proposed that we should be incorporating into competition law the principle of 'participative antitrust'.[10] Participation would allow industry to shape regulation, with the competition author- ities issuing co-developed guidelines, amenable to real-world testing, iteration and amendment.

As with any such scheme, though, the key is in determining who gets to participate, and as currently outlined the system seems to be ripe for capture by industry participants eager to have a hand in shaping the regulatory regime they are to oper- ate within. Instead, we should be consulting not just the company or companies involved, but also consumers, suppliers, workers, industry representatives, academia and civil society, such as consumer associations, trade unions and environmental

NGOs, to increase the relevance and legitimacy of antitrust policy and enforcement action.[11]

As one scholar notes, the role of the public is not to bring down particular companies but to participate 'both as complainant, litigant, critic, and catalyst for political change'.[12] A democratized system would have greater public oversight and consultation over which cases to bring, and public discussion of negotiated penalties and settlement agreements. This process of consultation is more common in Europe but there is scope there also to improve the level of access and influence for impacted parties. It is much more likely that regulators will have a good understanding of the changing market and competitive dynamics, especially in fast-moving industries, if they can rely on the support and cooperation of a range of stakeholders with diverse stores of industry information and the motivation to assist.

## Corruption and competence

Two of the most common objections to changing the consumer welfare standard are fears that going beyond the strictures of price and neoclassical economics opens antitrust up to politicization and also renders the system impossible to administer.

Before 2002, in the UK, the legal position was that mergers and monopolies were prohibited not if they reduced consumer welfare but if they operated against the 'public interest'. It was for the competition authorities to recommend enforcement action but the ultimate decision rested with the Secretary of State. This system suffered from unpredictability and political interference, and many practitioners were glad to see the modernization of UK competition law in line with the Chicago approach.

Interestingly, the politicization concern now raised by conservative antitrust thinkers does not tread the usual path of declaring that deep-pocketed corporations will capture the regulatory process. Rather, they argue on behalf of the well-resourced saying that the doors will be opened to all manner of political influence by unions and consumer representatives. This amounts to an objection that the lobbying playing field will be levelled and myriad stakeholder groups will also be able to influence regulators, as big corporates already do now.[13] It is also disingenuous: Chicago antitrust, with its preference for hands-off, light-touch regulation and its bias towards big business, is far from apolitical itself. The politics is already baked into the economics. To rebalance power in favour of those typically excluded from political action we must go at least a little out of our way to include them in the process – and to incorporate their concerns into the substance – of antitrust.

Concerns as to the administrability of stakeholder antitrust are also misplaced. The current ease of administering price-based analysis is achieved by systematically favouring big companies, and importing economic assumptions that really should be tested empirically – case by case – into law, rendering the underlying law ineffective. If dealing with diverse public interest issues becomes unwieldy, authorities and legislators can develop bright-line rules to aid with enforcement and compliance with the law.[14]

This does not mean we should adopt a less 'economic' or less 'scientific' approach, but it does involve recognizing that antitrust is a tool of both economic and social policy, therefore neoclassical economics and its desocialization of markets and economic actors is bound to fall short. As Robert Pitofsky warned in the late 1970s, 'it is bad history, bad policy, and bad law to exclude certain political values in interpreting the antitrust laws.'[15] Politics, political theory, political economy, sociology, anthropology, economic history, as well as the economics of industrial organization, institutional economics, and a broad church of feminist, ecological, cooperative and other erstwhile 'heterodox' branches of economics, should all be relevant to the antitrust inquiry.

## Stakeholder remedies

More robust enforcement will go some way towards dissipating power but, as we have seen, the shareholder value company by its very design seeks to accumulate power, so it is unlikely that antitrust will ever be able to keep up. There are also some industries which may naturally consolidate – where genuine economies of scale mean that the product is simply much better or cheaper when it is delivered at scale. In these cases, where vigorous antitrust enforcement alone cannot contain power, antitrust should step into the gap left by corporate law to impose responsibility on the most powerful companies to share any residual power that cannot be dispersed. The role of the competition authority would be to identify corporate power and thus to give power to those stakeholders subject to that corporate power.

Under stakeholder antitrust, the mere possession of power would be enough to trigger non-punitive 'stakeholder remedies', although the thresholds for triggering this remedy – how much power would have to be proven – will require careful thought and clear guidelines. Punitive fines breaking up companies and forcing companies to sell parts of their business would only be used when stakeholders are unable to exert sufficient influence over the company and where more competition might actually make the situation better.

Stakeholder remedies can be designed to achieve two separate but related aims:

1. remedying any immediate harm to stakeholders posed by a merger, commercial arrangement or conduct by a monopolistic company (for example, by conditioning

approval on the institution of measures to protect
consumer privacy or the environment); and

2. empowering stakeholders on an ongoing basis by
   shifting powerful companies away from the shareholder value model. Stakeholder remedies can give
   stakeholders rights to sue directors for breach of their
   new duties, or the ability to complain to a newly
   formed corporations regulator, with the ultimate
   prospect that the company could be dissolved for
   persistent and egregious transgressions.

It may, however, be the case that power to do harm sits not with
the individual company but with an entire industry. Many authorities are already empowered to look at such problems using what
is known as a 'market study'. The UK is one of only a few countries to have taken this concept further – the UK Competition and
Markets Authority is empowered not just to review a whole market or set of interrelated markets but also to enforce remedies.

Do competition authorities have the power to impose these
sorts of stakeholder remedies already? Stakeholder remedies
should be permissible under existing enforcement powers
although, as with other remedies, care must be taken to ensure
that they are not used as a way to sugar-coat or greenwash truly
harmful conduct: stakeholder remedies would not be a substitute for blocking a merger posing an anti-competitive threat, for
example, unless they adequately dealt with all competitive and
stakeholder concerns. The authorities must adhere to basic principles of rule of law and proportionality to avoid overreaching
their powers.[16]

The question of whether the courts would uphold remedies
going beyond the traditional antitrust enforcement repertoire
remains to be seen. But for those who predict a riot amongst companies and investors, it is interesting to note that, for example,
Facebook has effectively asked for just this sort of policing itself,
in terms of independent, stakeholder oversight, albeit without

the regulatory force and accountability of stakeholder antitrust.[17] And public companies in the UK are, as of recent reforms, already subject to requirements for employee representation at board level and the consideration of stakeholder interests.[18]

Stakeholder remedies, imposed as part of an antitrust case, will tend to be behavioural – requiring a change in the conduct of the company. There are a few precedents for stakeholder remedies along these lines. In the US, the Tesoro Corporation/BP PLC transaction in 2013 was approved subject to conditions limiting the ability of the company to lay off workers.[19] In 2011, the Federal Communications Commission made its approval of Comcast's NBCU acquisition conditional upon Comcast's commitment to subsidize broadband for low-income buyers.[20] In the UK, an investigation into the exchange of information between elite, fee-paying schools, begun as a result of whistle-blowing by two schoolboys who had hacked into the school computers and uncovered a trail of emails enticingly marked 'confidential',[21] concluded with a settlement agreement that included the establishment of a £3 million education trust for the benefit of students who may have been affected by the cartel.[22] In South Africa, the 2012 acquisition by Walmart of the leading local retailer, Massmart, was approved subject to Walmart reinstating the jobs of 503 people who had been fired just prior to the deal, freezing labour force reductions for two years, and establishing a R200 million (about £15 million) development fund to assist local producers in providing products to Walmart over the course of five years, with semi-annual reporting to the Competition Commission.[23]

Whilst these examples can be used for inspiration, none go so far as to change the nature of responsibility for powerful companies, as envisaged by stakeholder antitrust.

Behavioural remedies require ongoing monitoring by the regulator, although the burden will be lightened somewhat if stakeholders are given formal rights of oversight and influence within the company. Attempts to regulate companies by national authorities are naturally limited by the restrictions on jurisdictional reach and national sovereignty. These restrictions do not apply to stakeholders or civil society in general. Therefore, empowering stakeholders to pursue accountability through rights, access to information, voice, representation and influence can fill the gaps that occur in the patchwork of national enforcement, in lieu of greater international enforcement.

How much of a difference would stakeholder antitrust make? Companies currently take antitrust seriously because the fining and investigatory powers are extensive, and the possibility of the regulatory agency torpedoing the best-laid commercial plans of ambitious CEOs is ever present. Put simply, antitrust can get in the way of some of the things that shareholder value companies are built to do best: grow, acquire or merge with other companies, and attempt to oust rivals from the market by any means necessary. Modern antitrust represents an appropriate regulatory touch-point through which power and responsibility can be reunited, just as it once was under corporate law.

# 9.

## *Power to the people*

Corporate law has evolved over the centuries from the regulation of the right and privilege of incorporation through the imposition of public responsibility and the threat of dissolution of the company to a system with an almost exclusive focus on protecting the interests of shareholders and promoting shareholder value.

But if we are to give society a chance of counteracting corporate power then we must rethink the shareholder value corporation. Shareholder value demands that profits be maximized and distributed to shareholders. An alternative conception would be to democratize the corporation and to share the power of the company within the company itself, to co-opt the corporation's power and resources for the public good.

Competition will not serve society by itself; we must actively ensure that power is dispersed and shared. There will be absolute limits on the types of problems that corporations can help with, of course, but they can start by doing much less harm. We cannot continue to assume that corporate self-interest is a general, all-purpose tool for human betterment – and we must also recognize that, if companies are allowed to keep all the money and power they make on the road to success, they can use it to undermine our attempts at nudging them towards positive or even neutral impact.

## *Power to pull the plug*

It may be beyond the scope of competition regulators to oversee the implementation of stakeholder remedies, in particular where these remedies seek to give rights and power to specific stakeholders. We will explore in this chapter the mechanisms by which stakeholders can be empowered to contain, by themselves, the conduct of corporations, but there may also be a need to bolster the power of the state to challenge corporate power at a fundamental level, through some model of corporate chartering, with the concomitant power of the state to revoke the corporate charter under circumstances of persistent abuse and neglect. Before the twentieth century, companies were regularly dissolved in the public interest – indeed, before it was broken up under the Sherman Act, the Standard Oil Trust was challenged in just this way for breach of its Ohio charter.[1]

This is a model of corporate regulation with a long history – starting out in thirteenth-century England – but in fact the attorneys general of the individual US states still have the power to dissolve companies in the public interest.\* In the UK, where this model originated, the powers would have to be reintroduced. Currently, only a few organizations are formally chartered – both the Bank of England and the British Broadcasting Corporation have Royal Charters. The Secretary of State does have the power to petition the court to wind up any company for 'corporate abuse', including serious misconduct, fraud or 'sharp practices', but of the fifty-nine companies wound up on this basis in 2018/19, most were clear examples of financial scams.[2] The burst of over 350 companies wound up in the wake

\* Attorneys general have the power to bring what is called a *quo warranto* proceeding to challenge the actions of a corporation, and most US states have on their statute books a charter revocation law that allows for companies to be challenged in this way.

of the financial crisis perhaps shows some flexibility in our conception of what counts as a fraud against the public – what was previously thought of as financial wizardry was recast as deceit. But can we go further and mark the repeated and unconstrained negative spillovers of shareholder value as deception and fraudulence? Politicians in the UK are beginning to reach for such regulatory tools already – the Labour Party put forward a proposal that companies should be delisted from the London Stock Exchange if they do not adhere to environmental standards. This could have the equivalent effect of charter revocation.

## Stakeholder value mythology

What would responsible companies look like? How would they work? To replace the mythology of shareholder value we need a fresh story to succeed it – a new basis for the distribution of value and power within the corporate sector. The alternative is fairly obvious, although not without controversy. If externalities are disregarded by the firm, the best way to resolve the mismatch is by making companies internalize the costs.

According to the economist Ronald Coase – he of transaction costs fame – the free market would resolve any harm or misallocation of resources by itself, as long as someone was given the appropriate property rights. The polluter might be given the right to pollute, or the citizen might be given the right to clean air – either way, they would negotiate between themselves to the market optimal level of pollution.[3] But even Coase acknowledged that such bargaining can be highly problematic – how can millions of people, spread across the world, come together to bargain with a powerful polluter? In these circumstances the government would have to step in and tax the spillover-producing activity.

But there is also another way to protect the interests of stakeholders – by giving them not property rights per se but rights of influence and control over the company. As the Chief Economist of the Bank of England, Andy Haldane, explains:

> The most straightforward way of tackling embedded stakeholder externalities is to have those stakeholders' interests weighed explicitly in the objectives and decision-making of the company. In practical terms, that would mean modifying the objectives, rights and responsibilities of a firm under Company law.[4]

In short, no more shareholder value.

Instead of a model of redistribution of economic resources after all the money has been made and all the harm has been done, through regulation and taxation, we can encourage *pre-distribution* within the company, through corporate governance.[5] By involving society in the management of the corporation, and developing structures for broader participation, we can attempt to redirect the productive capacity of capitalism towards social good and change the bargaining position of the company in relation to the economy that supports it.

To allow stakeholders' interests to be 'weighed explicitly' would enable companies to internalize some of the social costs, and benefits, of their operations, empowering directors to consider spillovers – such as pollution, unemployment, lack of skills training – and the impact on local communities in their day-to-day duties.[6] This could be anything from reviewing the health effects of unhealthy products, taking into account the consequential cost of obesity or addiction, to adjusting production to reflect the cost of air purification and the treatment of childhood asthma due to unbreathable air.

But stakeholder value can also go beyond mitigation for economic costs: a company guided primarily by stakeholder interest may not just look at doing less harm but may even steer its profit generation towards products, services and operations that actively serve its communities and contribute to the public good. Such companies would continue to compete in the marketplace but, in theory, are no longer competing solely for profit – they are competing to best serve stakeholders.

At first it may seem onerous to ask companies to serve diverse groups of stakeholders, but in fact the point is to free companies from the shackles of shareholder servitude, allowing them to think about longer-term value creation. Just as few shareholder value companies actually succeed in maximizing shareholder value, stakeholder value companies may not successfully meet all stakeholders' needs or further all stakeholders' interests. But at least they will be working with and not against the grain of public benefit.

What happens when serving stakeholders requires trade-offs? One critique of stakeholder theory is that it is impossible for directors to maximize value in multiple directions; much better to stick with the single metric of long-term financial value, and to decide between stakeholder interests on that basis (similar to the 'enlightened shareholder value' model in the UK).[7] But as any parent of multiple children knows, maximization is a matter of perspective: I cannot give each of two children my maximum amount of attention – there will always be a trade-off, and toddlers seem to be uncanny in their ability to exploit this – but from the child's perspective it is possible for me to give the maximum amount of attention that they require. Trade-offs will still occur, but there is no logical impossibility. I can maximize 'value' for both of them, not from my perspective but from theirs.

Taking employee interests seriously, for example, does not mean failing to adopt technology that might replace them. It does however mean thinking about how to retrain and redeploy those workers, to use their knowledge of the production process to improve the new technology's sustainability credentials. The principle of 'just transition', which seeks to protect workers and communities from the costs of moving to a more environmentally sustainable economy, could be broadly applied to issues of stakeholder trade-off.

There is another concern that broadening the responsibilities of directors will allow them to escape responsibility altogether because they will always be able to claim that the interests of one group had to be sacrificed for another, creating a shield against scrutiny of their decisions. This is less an argument against stakeholder value, though, than it is against the current unenforceability of directors' duties in general. There are few mechanisms to hold directors accountable. But if stakeholder value is backed up with governance mechanisms to hold directors to account directly then management would not want to claim that shareholders' interests have been sacrificed in favour of workers, if this is not in fact the case – the workers will soon be at their door.

But won't investors flee to parts of the world where they are allowed to make profits unfettered by stakeholder value? If so, we should let them go, and use international channels to raise the standards around the world for people whose governments have forsaken them. Short of more robust international coordination on regulatory standards, which does not seem anywhere on the horizon, there will always be countries that find that their GDP is reliant on the abuse of corporate power, extraction of value and infliction of harm within their borders – whether the export of waste from the global north to the global south, or the global fast fashion supply chain that ends in a ravaged suburb of Dhaka. But this fearmongering – that all capital will flee if any restraint is placed on its profiteering – is loudest whenever there is a suggestion to enact labour laws that would have prevented Rana Plaza, or safety requirements that would have prevented Deepwater Horizon (indeed, the safety regulations enacted after the oil spill have since been rolled back).[8] In reality, there is an excess of money looking for investment. The whole thrust of stakeholder value is to empower global movements of stakeholders to counteract corporate power. Therefore, there may be nowhere for the most prominent companies to flee, as long as the most commercially important markets adopt this approach. If there are some investors who are determined to make as much money as they can, no matter what the cost to the rest of us, at least let us not willingly allow our economy, societies and habitats be turned into their financial playground. Let them go.

A related question is why anyone would choose to invest at all, if all the rents are to be pre-distributed? One answer to this is that shareholders are one constituency with which rents are to be shared, and they should receive some profit in return for investment. Another is that if individuals are not motivated to invest then communities and governments – local, national and supranational – may find themselves directing their own investment towards private sector provisions for public needs, where appropriate, in particular where the positive externalities of the product or service – like physical or digital infrastructure, transportation, payments or energy systems – render any investment good value for money because the benefits ripple out to society. We may see a collapse in investment by voracious global capital, which may hunker down into deep, dark pockets of the capitalist system, away from the real economy, but this will primarily affect the most extractive investment opportunities, which will no longer be appealing once the externalities and rent-seeking opportunities have been diminished. Pension funds, insurance companies and large public endowments will still need somewhere to put their money, and they will be doubly serving their beneficiaries by investing in the stakeholder economy, which brings returns in both income and public benefit.

## Stakeholder value companies

How can we share corporate power? There are some, but not many, existing models of companies attempting to move towards a model that serves broader interests.

At the time of my career crisis I realized that I had been push- ing frantically towards some undefined goal on the assumption that it would all be worth it in the end. But it did not feel worth it. So a friend challenged me to do something that felt pretty radical to me at the time: to stop pushing and to let go. I had quit my job in competition law but I stopped looking for another one. I opened my mind, reading things I would not normally read, taking in new information. All the while I was pondering the question of why it is that companies can create so much good and do so much harm at the same time. And that is when I stum- bled across B Corps – by wandering into a social event for responsible business and discovering an ambitious, passionate and welcoming movement of people trying to use business as a force for good.

B Corps – the 'B' stands for 'benefit', as in companies with public benefits – are a community of the world's top-perform- ing, certified ethical companies. For these companies, corporate responsibility is not just about good PR – they legally commit to having a material, positive impact on society and the environ- ment and must issue a 'Declaration of Interdependence' acknowledging that their corporate actions spark reactions, for which they are responsible. B Corps are certified by the non- profit B Lab as meeting its challenging standards for social and environmental impact. There are now around 2,500 B Corps globally.

As a competition lawyer, I was used to working with compa- nies that compete for profit alone, but here was a global community of successful businesses trying to serve not just the interests of shareholders but also the interests of their workers, communities and the planet. B Corps and other stakeholder models, like social enterprises and cooperatives, define the mission of the company around their diverse stakeholders, allowing them to integrate the interests of their workers, communities and the environment into company decision making.

Many companies wanting to become B Corps will have to change their form of incorporation so that they can move beyond shareholder value – especially in the US, where the shareholder value norm is strongest (in the UK, by contrast, companies can change their founding documents to achieve this). Otherwise, even if the law permits socially minded business, it does not require that the public interest should guide operations. Entrepreneurs can choose to do good but may find themselves under pressure to sell out – like Ben & Jerry's or craigslist.\* For those companies wanting to embed stakeholder value in their legal structure, the 'benefit corporation' model is available.[9] The 'benefit corporation' is a relatively new legal form which sits alongside the 'Inc.', 'LLC' and their equivalents in thirty-four states (plus Washington, DC) in the United States, Italy, Colombia and British Columbia (Canada). The benefit corporation is similar to the B Corp but without the robust certification. Over 5,000 companies have adopted benefit corporation status.

Companies across the economy, in a huge range of industries, have found different ways to best serve their stakeholders.

- Amalgamated Bank sees itself as America's socially responsible bank, investing in progressive and impactful causes and becoming a publicly traded company in order to expand its commitment to creating a more just, compassionate and sustainable planet.

---

\* Ben & Jerry's only became a B Corp after it was acquired by Unilever, and the decision to sell might have worked out differently if they had been a B Corp at the time of the takeover.

- COOK, a frozen food company making high-quality meals in the UK, chooses to employ ex-offenders in their kitchens.
- Public is a UK-based social design practice which launched the UK's first prison-based record label, InHouse Records, where all aspects of production take place within prisons. The aim is to empower inmates and prepare them for life after release.
- Fig Loans targets customers who cannot access mainstream credit and, instead of duping them into high-interest payday loans, it helps its customers rebuild their credit scores.
- Kresse Wesling MBE, who recycles decommissioned fire hoses into designer handbags and leather waste into woven rugs, says that she pursues profits because they are necessary to achieving her mission of reducing waste.
- Elephants Delicatessen in Portland, Oregon, rigorously tracks its contribution to community improvement, employee well-being and environmental protection, instead of just profits. The company has been going for 40 years, employs 450 people across 7 locations, and supplies wholesale products across the US. The deli donates tens of thousands of kilos of food that would otherwise go to landfill and all of its energy comes from renewable sources.
- Cascade Engineering is an engineered plastics manufacturer employing around 2,000 people, and since its inception in 1973 it has been a pioneer in pushing for social justice for minority groups.
- Patagonia, the outdoor clothing retailer, exhorts customers not to buy their jackets unless they really need to, and in 2017 the company filed a lawsuit against the United States government to prevent further incursions into protected national parks.

- Energy company Ørsted abandoned oil and gas for renewables. Now it has 11 offshore wind farms in the UK – including the world's biggest, which is capable of powering almost 600,000 UK homes.
- Kickstarter incorporated as a benefit corporation to help 'ensure that money – or the promise of it – would not corrupt their company's mission of enabling creative projects to be funded', in the words of their public announcement.
- Triodos Bank N.V., a certified B Corp and the largest ethical bank in the world, specifies its purpose in its articles of association as follows: 'With the exercising of banking business, the company aims to contribute to social renewal, based on the principle that every human being should be able to develop in freedom, has equal rights and is responsible for the consequences of his economic actions for fellow human beings and for the earth.'
- The Guardian Media Group has become the first major news organization to become a B Corp and has pledged to reach net zero emissions through its operations by 2030.

None of these companies will be perfect. Some are small-scale models that bigger companies can emulate, although some are also integrating 'business for good' on a large scale, like Danone North America (a business with a turnover of $5.5 billion) and Laureate Education, which was the first benefit corporation to go public, raising almost $500 million.

Today, stakeholder companies are like tenacious wild flowers, thriving in the cracks of the competitive capitalist rock face. They look outwards to their stakeholders to see how they can absorb energy, ideas, knowledge and resources, and work together to create shared value. But the main lesson from the 'profit with purpose' movement is that it is possible to do things differently; companies can generate profit and returns for share-holders whilst also looking out for workers, the community and the environment.

What the examples do show is that every industry, from energy to banking to clothing to food, is amendable to the stake-holder revolution. Repurposing companies by redirecting their efforts away from profits alone and towards the public interest has the potential to transform the private sector. The options for doing less harm and more good are limited only by corporate imaginations.

## Stakeholder governance

Stakeholder value is a model for corporate responsibility towards stakeholders built on the foundation of directors' duties – it relies on directors considering and serving stakeholder, and not just shareholder, interests. But what about empowering stake-holders to look after themselves?

In 1952, just as the Antitrust Project at the University of Chicago was getting under way, economist John Kenneth Galbraith published a book called *American Capitalism* in which he developed a theory of 'countervailing power'.[10] Galbraith observed that when industry consolidates towards monopoly, the disciplining force of competition is lost. But, he argued, the gap can be filled by countervailing power, not from other producers but from customers or suppliers. Big corporations need big unions with which to negotiate. Unions, far from destroying free market value, as Margaret Thatcher and my teenage self thought, create value by counterbalancing corporate power. Big suppliers do the same in relation to inputs, and big governments are needed to hold them all in check. The choice between big business and big government is shown to be unhelpful – to get the best out of either we need to have both.

Big corporations are not good in and of themselves, and therefore should not be left, unfettered, untethered, to grow bigger without restraint.

The Achilles heel of Galbraith's theory was his assumption that countervailing power was just as self-generating a regulatory force of market power as competition. But, in fact, just as competition needs to be actively safeguarded, so too must government and civil society be actively supported to countervail corporate power. Unions cannot balance big corporations if the rights of workers have been circumscribed. Civil society cannot tackle corporate misconduct if given no platform to do so. Smaller suppliers may not be able to offer a fairer alternative to customers if they are prevented by antitrust from cooperating.

One of the major issues with existing models of stakeholder companies is that few include mandatory governance structures for stakeholders. Without mechanisms to exert real influence over company actions, stakeholder value alone risks descending into a case of the powerful dictating the terms on which the powerless are to have their needs met. The most vocal critic along these lines has been Anand Giridharadas, who points to B Corps as yet another example of the rich, privileged elite self-selecting public causes to support in order to salve their consciences but without relinquishing control of the power and influence that come with their wealth.[11]

Stakeholder value creates a responsibility for company directors to internalize stakeholder interests and pre-distribute the economy's resources, but this should be more than a simple mantra like 'Don't be evil', which Google has since removed as its motto. It should be complemented by stakeholder governance that seeks to give more power to the powerless.

Some companies already do this, for example, through 'Mission Councils', like at Pukka Teas (a subsidiary of Unilever);[12] by having stakeholder representatives on the board, like at Divine Chocolate, where Ghanaian cocoa farmers are board members;[13] or by having an employee-elected council to liaise with management, as at Aviva plc.[14] Companies may also bring their investors along for the ride, through models of investment such as Toast Ale's 'Equity for Good'[15] – where shareholders commit to channel their capital gains into further stakeholder enterprises – and Danone's pioneering $2 billion syndicated credit facility in which the company's cost of capital will vary with its environmental and social impact.[16]

The shareholder value model of the business firm was so successful that many other forms of business organization have been woefully underexplored. Cooperative ownership has thrived all around the world but the scale and adoption of the model remains unnecessarily limited. When Richer Sounds, the UK hi-fi and TV retail chain, became employee-owned in 2019, it joined a list of only around 350 such companies in the UK, including John Lewis, the biggest employee-owned company in the UK with turnover of over £10 billion. The remote communities of the far-flung islands off the Scottish coast have a long history of community cooperatives, built from a need for self-reliance and pooling of resources, but the same model has not been attempted more widely. Cooperatives reverse the trend of annexing public wealth into private hands and instead embody values of shared wealth, community, mutual respect and dignity in work. There is plenty of room for further experimentation throughout the economy.

We can also take inspiration from other, more stakeholder-friendly jurisdictions. Germany is one of the world leaders in stakeholder governance, especially in relation to workers, with a system called 'co-determination'. Under the Anglo-American model, companies tend to have one board, whose chairman is often also the chief executive officer (CEO), employees have little or no say in strategy, and the directors usually believe that their responsibility is to act in the interests of shareholders. Large German companies, by contrast, have two boards – the *Vorstand*, or executive board, and the *Aufsichtsrat*, or supervisory board. The supervisory board is responsible for the selection, appointment, dismissal and, of course, supervision of the executive board. Around half of the members of the supervisory board of very large joint-stock companies are chosen by shareholders, the other half are elected by workers, and there will generally also be bank representatives on the supervisory board as well. At the other end of the scale, every factory with at least five regular employees is entitled to elect a works council, which has the right to negotiate key issues with management, including the hiring of new employees, the introduction of new technology, use of overtime and, in the case of redundancies, the negotiation of redeployment, severance payments and early retirement.

Far from torpedoing the productivity and profitability of companies, evidence shows the neutral or positive effects of co-determination and works councils on each.[17] On the other hand, as one would expect, shareholder returns are lower and wages are higher – reflecting the different balance of power between capital and labour, with labour claiming its share of available economic rents.[18]

Introducing one group of stakeholders into the decisional mix does not correct for all personality flaws of a profit-seeking business: Volkswagen and its fellow German car makers are each subject to the requirements of co-determination but the drive for profits led these companies not only to cheat regulators' emissions tests in order to pass off polluting cars as clean but also to collude with each other to prevent cleaner technology from entering the market.[19] One might wonder how this could have happened with stakeholder involvement at board level but then co-determination requires only input from workers, not from environmental groups or consumer associations, and workers may have their own profit motive.

It may be that changing the structure of the board is the only way to introduce the voices of representatives who can credibly represent a broad range of stakeholders.[20] Boards of large companies tend currently to be made up of senior management and large shareholders. Employee representatives can be chosen by the workforce, along the German model, and community leaders could be given advisory roles. The Dutch model provides for the nomination of a 'public interest director', whose responsibility is to vet company decisions from the standpoint of the public, and this may be the best way to channel the views of long-term business partners, suppliers and creditors also. Representatives could join the executive board – although, to make this effective, this will require the disclosure of commercial and sensitive information, with confidentiality restrictions, to enable the representatives to accurately represent stakeholder views and feed back to their constituencies.

One of the advantages of stakeholder governance is that it creates a regulatory check within the company itself, ideally giving voice to consumers, workers, local residents and public interest groups, as well as investors. This has distinct benefits, because stakeholders are generally better motivated, have more information and have the global reach to monitor corporate conduct beyond the resource and jurisdictional limits of any national regulator. This creates a democratized and decentralized system of governance, allowing for tailored and more creative solutions.

## Stakeholder enforcement

Accountability is a huge issue, given the opportunity for 'greenwashing'. Stakeholders are alive to this, as Coca-Cola discovered when its 'PlantBottle', marketed as an environmentally friendly alternative to a traditional plastic bottle, was found to contain only 15 per cent plant-based materials.[21] B Corps are not immune to this either: in 2016, lab tests commissioned by the *Wall Street*

*Journal* found that detergent products produced by The Honest Company, a certified B Corp founded by actress Jessica Alba, contained a harmful chemical that the company had claimed it did not use.[22] Public disclosure and standardized reporting would go some way towards remedying this.

But it is difficult even for shareholders to enforce shareholder value, so it is not clear that stakeholders would fare any better even if they were given the right to sue for stakeholder value, which current models like the benefit corporation do not contemplate.[23] There would be an important role for the newly formed corporations regulator to investigate complaints by stakeholders and to bring cases on behalf of stakeholders unable to bring their own claims.

An independent corporations regulator, with investigative and enforcement powers, would be able to monitor stakeholder remedies devised by competition authorities but would also be able to regulate in its own right, imposing responsibilities and limits on the most powerful companies in the economy. Elizabeth Warren's Accountable Capitalism Act envisions the recreation of an Office of United States Corporations at the Department of Commerce, and the Institute of Public Policy Research has proposed the creation of a Companies Commission in the UK.[24]

In Australia, the Australian Securities and Investments Commission (ASIC) has the power to bring proceedings for a breach of directors' duties and has done so in several cases.[25]

The creation of a public regulator would provide much-needed public oversight and a more robust process than relying on Congress to rake Mark Zuckerberg over the coals – a privilege not yet enjoyed by the UK and other countries – or trusting MPs to grill Philip Green over the BHS collapse, in each case after the relevant scandal had broken. But the ultimate threat would be revocation of the corporate charter or dissolution of the company for repeated and persistent disruption of the public interest.

There are big questions that remain unanswered about how stakeholder value would work, in general – and in relation to powerful companies, in particular. Which stakeholders are relevant, and therefore should be included? Which are the most important, and therefore should be given greater weight? What should be the role of the regulator – actively monitoring markets or just responding to complaints? How can any regulator have sufficient information to engage with such an exercise effectively? What happens if multinational companies are subject to very different standards of stakeholder value in different countries? We do not have satisfactory answers to these questions, not least because we have paid them hardly any attention, relative to the colossal human effort expended in the past decades in business schools, law schools, economics departments and management training on the single question of how to maximize profit. If we were to embark on a stakeholder antitrust, stakeholder value and stakeholder governance journey, as this book very much hopes that we do, then the answers would likely evolve through experience, practice and the mass of research needed to fill this scholarly gap.

## Stakeholder infrastructure

The broader vision proposed in this book is for a market-embedded infrastructure of stakeholder participation. The institutions of our economic system must be radically transformed to respond to the climate crisis, technological threat and democratic failure, and to create an entirely new path through which power and money can flow through the economic system towards people, communities and movements at large. Especially as we stare climate and social collapse in the face, we must create and embed this new infrastructure of power now, else there may be no mechanism for doing so if the worst were to happen.

Beyond strengthening governance and enforcement, there are several other measures that would support the adoption of stakeholder value and stakeholder governance as part of stakeholder antitrust.

For one thing, a clarification in the law, bringing it in line with modern practices, would help dispel the lingering uncertainty over corporate responsibility. To address the legacy of the Bishop of Oxford case in the UK, a coalition of charities is seeking a new ruling in 2019 that charities should be aligning their investment policies with their charitable aims, not just focusing on maximizing returns.[26] If successful, this could read across into corporate law, bolstering the requirements of the Companies Act for stakeholder interests to be taken into account in company decision making.

It is a tall order to expect that stakeholders will readily be able to bargain with companies if just given the formal rights to do so. There is a long tradition amongst unions of training up representatives from early in their careers – much as politicians do circuits of local politics before heading for national government. National programmes of training would support stakeholders unfamiliar with negotiating in the corporate world, and the biggest companies could be required to fund this.

Unlike as is currently the case in politics, it would be useful to have a more representative group of people actually running companies. Currently executives rotate between companies, exchanging leadership roles amongst a relatively tight elite. But sometimes it can take having a completely different background to bring a fresh perspective. The recently appointed Digital Minister in Taiwan is a former hacker, for whom the mutual back-scratching between government and the private sector is anathema. She has instituted a policy of radical transparency – livestreaming all 'private' meetings she has with companies and representatives, with transcripts immediately available online.[27] Such an idea to tackle corruption would not occur to someone who came from the same social circles as other ministers and executives. Allowing members of the public to gain some insight into corporate administration, perhaps through some kind of corporate participation or board duties – allocated more or less at random, just like jury service – would give the public some access to corporate decision making, and vice versa.

Participation in general could become a stronger part of democratic and societal involvement in business, with infrastructure put in place for civil society and communities to pool ideas, resources, knowledge and public power as a counterbalance to the private power of companies, and to inform and coordinate interactions with and influence over government. Broader schemes for place-based local development – such as the transatlantic Community Wealth Building initiatives – are mutually supportive of stakeholder value and stakeholder governance, as they encourage democratic and active participation, citizen control, collective ownership and sustainable development.[28]

Another supporting mechanism for stakeholder value and stakeholder governance is to actually increase the influence that shareholders have over companies by broadening ownership – i.e. making good on Margaret Thatcher's vision of a 'nation of shareholders' – and also making it easier for individuals to direct their pension funds to invest in stakeholder companies. The Labour Party's proposals for inclusive ownership funds for workers – into which all companies in the UK with over 250 employees would be forced to transfer 10 per cent of shares – are aimed at allowing workers to receive a share of the gains in corporate profit they already help to create. The vast majority of everyday shareholders have almost no influence over how the companies they invest in are run, so strengthening the link between shareholders' actual interests, which are not always solely financial, and corporate action would also be beneficial. The government can also support stakeholder value through its own procurement. If companies are able to 'gain credit' in public tenders for the public benefits they create, this can act as an incentive or signal, nudging companies towards social good.

## Responsible bigness

Making stakeholder value mandatory for all companies would establish a baseline for corporate capitalism, but there is also a risk that standards would slip down to the lowest common denominator. It would be better to make corporate responsibility proportionate to the size, complexity and power of corporations. Instead of having regulators and stakeholders enforcing stakeholder value on all companies, we can place our focus where the problems are most intractable, the bargaining positions most imbalanced, and the potential for change the biggest: where there is power. If a company wins the race to dominance and its only responsibility is to make more money, this incentive and behaviour will then filter throughout the whole market – as it has, in fact, done. If, however, powerful companies are held to account for their full impacts on society, this will then become the new market expectation.

This is the aim of Elizabeth Warren's Accountable Capitalism Act, which requires corporate chartering for companies with over $1 billion in turnover. Similarly, the French 'vigilance' law mandates the identification, prevention and mitigation of human rights violations and significant environmental harm by large companies only and creates civil liability to compensate stakeholders for harms that could have been avoided. The duty is owed by the companies themselves, not their directors, and is owed to the public.

Those who oppose regulation in general often argue – as another Chicago School stalwart, George Stigler, did in 1971 –

that 'as a rule, regulation is acquired by the industry and is designed and operated primarily for its benefit'.[29] This is a classic 'blame the victim' approach: it is the government's fault that it gets captured by big business; therefore, the neoliberal solution is to reduce the size of government, rather than decreasing the size, influence and excess profits of business. The evidence does show that business indeed captures government, but it is big business doing the capturing in order to keep small potential rivals out of the market.[30] Regulations and responsibilities should be primarily aimed at incumbents, who can afford them, not companies just getting started, and we might consider placing an ultimate cap on the size of industry – Zephyr Teachout suggests that companies worth over $10 billion should lose limited liability.[31]

Using corporate size as a trigger for supervision is a good start, but it may not capture all concerns. It is also a missed opportunity to recalibrate competitive capitalism by tying power to responsibility.

In fact, EU competition law already does give more responsibility to certain companies, based on power. For example, dominant companies have a 'special responsibility' not to distort competition in the EU, and German law contains the concept of 'relative' market power. More recent proposals to level the playing field between the antitrust authorities and the Big Tech companies, in particular, have considered the relevance of power to the assessment – for example, the proposal to single out companies with 'strategic market status' for greater scrutiny.[32]

Why should we assume that stakeholder-centric companies will not pursue power, just as shareholder value companies do? Perhaps they will. Certainly, having workers on boards has not stopped companies like Volkswagen from seeking market strength. But what power such companies are able to glean will be shared among the stakeholders and directed accordingly. And we might hope that, if there is comprehensive representation for communities, suppliers, civil society and government, it will be less likely that crushing or excluding a rival or making money, no matter what the risks, will be seen by the board as a manifestly good business plan.

# Conclusion

When Guy Singh-Watson was honoured in 2019 with the 18th Award for Responsible Capitalism, presented by Princess Anne, he found himself getting angry. Singh-Watson runs Riverford Organic, an organic vegetable delivery service, which he grew from a one-wheelbarrow business to a company serving 50,000 customers every week. Whilst he appreciated the impulse to recognize the responsible efforts of business leaders, he lamented the lack of any sense of urgency to change the way things are done. Singh-Watson used his 3 minutes at the podium, in front of 200 ambassadors, lords and powerbrokers, to give an angry speech about the failures of capitalism. He told them:

> We have created a system designed to make us behave irresponsibly, and then abdicated personal responsibility for our actions with the excuses that we are just 'following the rules', 'doing what others do', 'being realistic'. Capitalism has made it normal and acceptable to profit from destroying our collective future. Bizarrely, economists and policymakers present this paradigm as rationality; to me it seems pathologically delusional.[1]

The audience seemed to agree, but they also seemed out of touch with the scale of the problem. One woman told him that she could see climate change happening at first hand, because she had to walk a bit further from her ski chalet to the retreating glacier. He was told that 'we need more people like you', to which he later wrote in reply that we actually need more people like the people at the award ceremony, with the option to change their ways and the power to set a better example. Guy wrote to his customers that:

> . . . we will only solve the problem when those with power and wealth accept their responsibilities to the rest of humanity, changing their values and their behaviour. Responsibility for our collective future must underpin every decision, rather than being an afterthought at the end of a successful career, or a reluctant concession to protect brand value. It cannot be secondary to profit.[2]

In 2018, Singh-Watson sold Riverford Organic to his employees, which was probably the action that gained him the award. He sold the company for a quarter of its market value on the basis that £6 million is more than enough for one person and, 'Only a fool would think that £24 million would make you any happier than £6 million'. He reports that the day he handed over the company he had built over thirty years to his staff was the happiest day of his life. One of his employees turned to him at the celebratory party and said, 'We are creating a little piece of the world I have always wanted to live in.'

## From power to possibility

What has been missing from the discussion of how to reform capitalism is an understanding of how free market competition and shareholder value reinforce each other, leading to unintended consequences. It turns out that, when you tie the powerful engine of competition to the shareholder value corporation, you get a machine that is designed to eat the world, and get big doing so. A desire to beat their rivals is what drove Facebook or Amazon or Uber to create products and services people love. But free market competition also allows them to use the power that they gain over the market to design their products in ways that generate more profit at the expense of society, and there are few checks and balances that they cannot evade or manipulate with their market domination. Power should not be ignored, and responsibility should not be abdicated. If we are to rebalance capitalism, we must find a way to share power and internalize externalities.

For many, the challenges of this generation and the generations to come are overwhelming, heartbreaking and depressing. That we have ended up in this position largely of our own making adds to the sense of bewilderment. We still cannot answer the simple questions of economics (what we shall produce, by whom, and who gets to consume it) in a way that makes sense for our future on this planet.

We know that something is wrong, that we cannot continue as we are, and that many of us are complicit. We each have our own totems of truth – the little nuggets of information that we file away in our minds as reminders that the dominant paradigm is failing us. You will have your own. For me it has been Rana Plaza, the Cambridge Analytica data breach, the global financial crisis, and fizzy drinks. It is also the accumulation and compounding of smaller humiliations, injustices and inhumanities, which people around the world are asked daily to accept as the price of progress. We can ignore the truth no longer.

For complex and multi-faceted problems like inequality, arguably the time has come to pull all the levers. Yes, we can introduce or reinforce minimum wage laws, yes, we should support the re-empowerment of unions, yes, we should redistribute wealth. But this is like turning all the taps on at full blast to fill up the bathtub, without plugging up the drain. Companies that manage to compete their way to market power, bringing with it economic power and political power, and under the spell of shareholder value pushing them to seek further economic rents, will continue to siphon off resources from the common pool.

We can attempt to address issues of biodiversity, nutrition, sustainability, farmers' and indigenous rights in the agricultural sector through regulation, but it is naive to look at these issues as separate to the trend of mass consolidation and the reality of just four global agribusiness players. Instead, zeroing in on the most powerful actors through stakeholder antitrust, and forcing these companies to allow stakeholders into the boardroom, provides a path towards rebalancing power in the economy and society. This, as well as efforts to broaden the shareholding base amongst everyday shareholders, preventing further consolidation and introducing more competition into the market, recirculates the water back into the tub instead of letting it drain away.

Our current approach towards regulating corporate power is disjointed, and allows plenty of power to slip through the cracks, because we have failed to connect two separate policy conversations: about corporate power and monopoly, on the one hand, and corporate responsibility and stakeholder capitalism, on the other.

Competition authorities are uniquely placed to make sure markets are working well for everyone. Figuring out how competition works in specific industries is their bread and butter. But if, as it is sometimes supposed, the authorities are not up to the job with the resources and expertise that they have now – especially once their remit is expanded to embrace stakeholder antitrust – then let's get them what they need.

Antitrust must have something to say about the rising levels of economic concentration and the consolidation of power into fewer and fewer hands. Antitrust traditionalists fear the populist takeover of the discipline, but they should really be worried about its increasing irrelevance. One prominent economist told me that they had been involved in over 200 mergers over their 30-year career, and not one of them had anything good going for it, other than for shareholders and executives. But if the vast majority of mergers fail to successfully integrate and realize efficiencies, even for the merging parties, and prices are going up regardless of the limited interventions of competition agencies, we have to ask ourselves: how can antitrust contribute in any meaningful way if it continues to be in the thrall of big business?

I left antitrust practice in 2013, after the catastrophic Rana Plaza collapse and my fizzy drinks epiphany, but I came back to the field because I see an opportunity to materially change the way we regulate markets in order to address the need to reorient all our systems towards sustainability in all its meanings. There are others who also see an opening for new ways of doing things: from Kate Raworth's Doughnut Economics movement, B Corps, the Institute of New Economic Thinking, and student movements like Rethinking Economics, to cooperatives and community groups, the C40 cities, the circular economy, Extinction Rebellion, and the growing movement of antitrust scholars and advocates shaking the discipline to attention.

Climate change, geopolitical instability, resource security, migration – these problems are not going away. If we do not involve business in fixing them, and treat it as the enemy, to be suppressed and sidelined, then we give business a free pass: we absolve it of its moral and economic responsibility to remedy the damage that it, in part, caused. But we also pass up the opportunity to access the vast resources at its disposal – not only cash and investments but also the millions of talented and resourceful people currently employed by private enterprises.

Power was once part of the discussion. We can bring it back. And we can go further. The understanding of power in the 1940s was of its own time: it was before our climate change awakening, before globalization, before outsourcing, before the global financial crisis, before computers, mobile phones and the internet, before social media, before mass urbanization, before the crest of the civil rights movement in the US, before the formation of the European Coal and Steel Community (the predecessor to the EU), and before millions of people ceased farming just for themselves and entered the formal, global workforce. We can update our understanding of power and the role that corporations play in it for the twenty-first century. We have the science and economics, now, to prove that deregulation of industry is disastrous for the planet. But we can also be open about the political agenda: to build a fairer, sustainable, survivable world in which companies cannot ride roughshod over people's lives and futures for the sake of shareholder returns.

The lesson from the financial crisis, and the trillions spent in bailouts, was surely that when any commercial organization gets 'too big to fail' its impact on the market can blot out the market itself. This means we must also broaden our understanding of the power of big companies in order to reinstate the connection with responsibility. As long as we have markets, there will always be pockets of private power that seek to subvert the economic system and extract publicly created value for themselves. We may never be able to stop this, certainly not with companies designed as they are today. But we can share the power around. And if we do not, we may lose control of big companies completely.

All companies should be given the permission, and some the obligation, to deploy their ample resources towards solving global problems. With 85 per cent of people worldwide dissatisfied with their jobs,[3] people within companies are looking for purpose too. We are facing twin realities: the window for surviving the damage we are doing to the planet is closing and the runway for affecting the trajectory of our economic and technological development is running out. These global challenges present new opportunities for those stuck in the rat race to stop what they are doing right now and get stuck into the twenty-first century's most urgent projects. At the same time, corporations have $19 trillion sitting on their balance sheets as savings. It is time to put that money to work.

# Afterword

This book is important. Agree with it or not: do not ignore it. Many ideas here may appear radical but not only are they a very timely call for reflection and action, they include many ideas that are likely to become mainstream in the future – and let's hope, for the sake of the planet and society, that that future is not too far off. Already many young lawyers – and some not so young – are crying out for a more realistic approach to both competition law/antitrust and the control of corporate power more generally. Many vote with their feet – or rather, their brains – and will no longer join firms with a narrow, outdated focus on profit, whatever the cost. As Michelle says: 'We are many, seeking new and better answers, and we are not giving up.' Not since I read Kate Raworth's *Doughnut Economics* have I felt such a need to rethink our approach to so many important issues facing society.[1] Now is not the time to be timid!

In a book that is highly informed and enjoyable to read, Michelle challenges current conventional thinking and tackles issues of power, inequality and social harm directly, rejecting highly theoretical ideas that so-called 'free' markets will some-how sort these out – fully recognizing that these markets are not really 'free', being the result of a series of complex policy and regulatory choices.

She explodes a multitude of myths, particularly the idea that the market is a given and that outcomes and prices determined by that market must automatically be the right ones. She reveals so-called 'externalities' for what they are – costs avoided by companies and paid for by us, as citizens: 'These harms to society and environment, which are not priced by the market system, accrue within the economic system anyway, acting as a lead weight dragging society and the economy down.' Externalities are seen as a source of undeserved profits in the form of costs that the company does not have to pay, and exploitation of these rents is a form of unfair competition.

Whilst we may object that some externalities, such as education of the workforce, should properly be borne by society as a whole, she is right that, if companies are to make the right choices consistent with a fair and sustainable future, many of these costs should be borne by companies and reflected in their pricing accordingly. Pollution by lorries and factories and energy choices are good examples. Certainly we have a very incomplete measure of 'efficiency' if so many costs are simply not taken into account.

The discussion of stakeholder antitrust helpfully reminds us what a corporation or company really is – and what it is not. Whilst they have been extremely useful vehicles for the development of ideas, technology, goods and services, it is important to remember that they are just that – useful vehicles. They are not real, living things – even if there is a trend towards attributing 'human' rights to them. They are a man-made artefact; 'a publicly granted privilege allowed only at the sufferance of the state'. Privileges, including limited liability, can be withdrawn – or at least made conditional. It is doubtful that companies ever owed a duty only to shareholders but it is certainly the case that, as a society, we should think carefully about who companies owe duties to. Why should shareholders' interests be privileged over those of the planet, the environment or employees – many of whom will often have more invested in the company than many shareholders? Michelle's book is full of ideas about how to find a sane and practical balance between these interests – in both the law and in the running of a modern, efficient, profitable and sustainable business.

Governments around the world are struggling with the problem of 'big data' and the so-called FANGs (Facebook,

Amazon, Netflix and Google). At the heart of this discussion is the issue of corporate power and how (or whether) to control it. The scope of Michelle's book is much wider than this and reminds us of antitrust's original concern over power; it makes a powerful plea to refocus on power – rather than price – and makes a series of proposals to contain it. As Michelle recognizes, much more work needs to be done in this area, but this book pushes us to ask the right questions. Who has power? How was it obtained? How is it being used/abused? What should be the thresholds for intervention? What form should remedies take – break up, removal of limited liability, greater stakeholder control?

Michelle's analysis makes it inevitable that sustainability should cease to be at the 'fringe of modern competition law' but become an integral part of it. This fits with my own plea in relation to the existential threat posed by climate change: 'competition law must be part of the solution, not part of the problem'.[2] However, Michelle's call for stakeholder antitrust goes much further and to the very heart of what we expect from a system of corporate law and competition law, and what it means to be a good corporate citizen.

In some respects Michelle's experience parallels my own: working in private practice in the City of London, with a growing realization of the disconnect between the technocratic practice of competition law and the things that really matter. I spent thirty-five years as a practitioner, leading a large global practice for many years, constrained to follow the conservative decisional practice and guidance of the competition authorities and, whilst trying not to be risk averse, nevertheless constrained to give advice that reflected that conservative practice.

Now, as an academic and judge, I have a greater freedom. As an academic, I can say what I think the law ought to be if it is leading to outcomes which are either unfair or incompatible with a sustainable future. As a judge at the UK's Competition

Appeal Tribunal, I am still free to disagree with Commission guidelines but, ultimately, we are obliged to follow the treaties and the rulings of the higher courts – especially those of the Court of Justice of the EU (CJEU).

Happily, the more I look at the EU Treaties, especially what I term the 'constitutional' provisions – i.e. the bits at the beginning of those treaties setting out their objectives and instructing us how to apply the rest of them – the more I realize that they are entirely consistent with an approach to competition law that takes full account of the environment and sustainability. What is more, they say these 'must' be taken into account in 'all' the EU's policies and activities. Just take a look again at Article 3(3) of the Treaty on European Union* and Articles 7, 9 and 11 of the Treaty on the Functioning of the European Union (TFEU).**

Against this background it is morally reprehensible that competition law has often failed us. It has failed us with an unnecessarily narrow focus on financial considerations and price effects. It has failed us by not factoring in sustainability, either properly or fully. Some well-intentioned attempts have been made to do so, but these have often fallen short. A good example is the 'Chicken of Tomorrow' case, which Michelle discusses. Here the Dutch competition authority tried to support

---

*Article 3 (3) reads: 'The Union . . . shall work for the sustainable development of Europe based on balanced economic growth and price stability, a highly competitive social market economy, aiming at full employment and social progress, and a high level of protection and improvement of the quality of the environment.'

** Article 7 requires the Union to 'ensure consistency between its policies and activities, taking all of its objectives into account'; Article 9 to ensure 'the promotion of a high level of employment, the guarantee of adequate social protection, the fight against social exclusion, and a high level of education, training and protection of human health'; Article 11 to maintain a commitment 'to promoting sustainable development'.

industry efforts to improve animal welfare but failed to do so – probably because it placed too much weight on subjective views, on short-term price factors, and too little weight on the interests of future consumers and society as a whole, to say nothing of the poor chickens.

Competition law has also failed to contain the increasing concentration seen in many markets and industries and, at least in the US, has failed to have the courage to act against abuses by, for example, large technology companies. There are signs of change in the US, with recent studies by the FTC, and increasing interest in corporate power in the Democratic Party. It remains to be seen, however, how this will play out.

The tragedy is that the competition authorities already have the mandate and tools to deal with all these issues – for example, in the 'constitutional' provisions of the EU Treaties to which I have already referred. These tools have been used very effectively in the past – as we have seen in cases like the Commission's decision in the CECED case relating to energy-efficient washing machines (in which the Commission allowed an agreement between importers and manufacturers to stop marketing energy inefficient machines). However, they need to be used more often and with more confidence. As the French might say: *'Courage, mon brave, courage!'* The authorities should stop obsessing over arcane concepts that are *not* in the treaties, such as consumer welfare – at least the wrongly conceived, narrow price-centric version of it – and refocus on what *is* in the EU Treaties and what they say the competition authorities 'must' do.

In my recent work, I have stuck strictly to what the treaties permit – indeed, to what they require. Much of what Michelle advocates can be achieved within the limits of competition law and corporate law as it stands – at least in countries like the UK, where company law already requires companies to take into account interests wider than those of shareholders, and companies can set out their objectives in their founding documents.

That said, Michelle also sets out a number of bold ideas that go beyond the limits of current law. But that is a good thing. Yes, changing the law often takes a long time, but the concerns Michelle raises are very real. Her ideas merit serious attention at the highest level and by those in power.

Simon Holmes
Member of the UK's Competition Appeal Tribunal
Academic Visitor  at the Centre for Competition Law and
Policy, Oxford University

# Endnotes

## Preface: Changing my mind about the free market

1 Human Rights Watch, *'Whoever Raises their Head Suffers the Most':
Workers' Rights in Bangladesh's Garment Factories*, report published
22 April 2015.
2 Sarah Labowitz, '"We have one eye open and one eye closed": The
dirty labor secrets of fast fashion', *Ideas*, 24 April 2017.

## 1 Competition by any other name

1 Statista, 'The 100 largest companies in the world by market value
in 2019 (in billion U.S. dollars)': https://www.statista.com/
statistics/263264/top-companies-in-the-world-by-market-value/
(accessed January 2020).
2 Matthew Garrahan, 'Google and Facebook dominance forecast to
rise', *Financial Times*, 4 December 2017.
3 Jeff Desjardins, 'The Tech Takeover of Advertising in One Chart',
*Visual Capitalist*, 22 September 2017.
4 Hannah Kuchler, 'How Facebook grew too big to handle', *Financial Times*, 28 March 2019.
5 Trucost plc, *Natural Capital at Risk – The Top 100 Externalities of Business*, report undertaken on behalf of the TEEB for Business
Coalition and released at a Business for the Environment summit
in New Delhi, April 2013.
6 Trefis Team, 'AmEx Is Likely To Become The Second Largest U.S.
Card Processing Company This Year', *Forbes*, 29 May 2018; Financial

Conduct Authority, 'Market overview' in *Credit card market study: MS14/6*, interim report published 3 November 2015.

7  OECD, *Concentration in Seed Markets: Potential Effects and Policy Responses*, study published 4 December 2018, p. 19.

8  OECD, *Concentration in Seed Markets*, p. 10.

9  Jonathan Tepper, *The Myth of Capitalism: Monopolies and the Death of Competition*, John Wiley & Sons, 2018, p. 123.

10  Tepper, *The Myth of Capitalism*, p. xvii.

11  Resolution Foundation, *Is everybody concentrating? Recent trends in product and labour market concentration in the UK*, report published 26 July 2018.

12  Scott Corfe and Nicole Gicheva, *Concentration not competition: the state of UK consumer markets*, Social Market Foundation, October 2017.

13  Gustavo Grullon, Yelena Larkin and Roni Michaely, 'Are U.S. Industries Becoming More Concentrated?', *Review of Finance*, 25 October 2018.

14  Tommaso Valletti, 2019 (unpublished paper). For more on rising concentration across North America and Europe, see OECD Productivity Working Paper No. 18, 'Industry Concentration in Europe and North America', published January 2019.

15  Bruce A. Blonigen and Justin R. Pierce, 'Evidence for the Effects of Mergers on Market Power and Efficiency', NBER Working Paper No. 22750, October 2016.

16  John E. Kwoka, *Mergers, Merger Control, and Remedies: A Retrospective Analysis of U.S. Policy*, MIT Press, 2014.

17  See Simcha Barkai's 2016 paper for the University of Chicago, 'Declining Labor and Capital Shares'; Jason Furman and Peter Orszag, 'A Firm-Level Perspective on the Role of Rents in the Rise in Inequality', presented at 'A Just Society' Centennial Event in Honor of Joseph Stiglitz, Columbia University, New York, NY, 16 October 2015; Germán Gutiérrez and Thomas Philippon, 'Declining Competition and Investment in the U.S.', NBER Working Paper No. 23583, July 2017.

18 See Jan De Loecker and Jan Eeckhout, 'The Rise of Market Power and the Macroeconomic Implications', NBER Working Paper No. 23687, August 2017; Jan De Loecker and Jan Eeckhout, 'Global Market Power', NBER Working Paper No. 24768, June 2018.

19 See Barkai, 'Declining Labor'.

20 *World Inequality Report 2018*, originally presented at the inaugural WID.world conference at the Paris School of Economics on 14 December.

21 Oxfam Briefing Paper, 'Public Good or Private Wealth', published January 2019.

22 Leader article, 'Overhaul tax for the 21st century', *The Economist*, 9 August 2018.

23 Emmanuel Saez and Gabriel Zucman, 'Wealth Inequality in the United States since 1913: Evidence from Capitalized Income Tax Data', NBER Working Paper No. 20625, October 2014.

24 Josh Bivens, 'The Top 1 Percent's Share of Income from Wealth has Been Rising for Decades', Economic Policy Institute, 23 April 2014.

25 Edward N. Wolff, 'Household Wealth Trends in the United States, 1962 to 2016: Has Middle Class Wealth Recovered?', NBER Working Paper No. 24085, November 2017.

26 Joshua Gans et al., 'Inequality and Market Concentration, When Shareholding is More Skewed than Consumption', NBER Working Paper No. 25395, December 2018.

27 Sean F. Ennis, Pedro Gonzaga and Chris Pike, 'The Effects Of Market Power On Inequality', *Competition Policy International*, 14 October 2017.

28 Gabriel Zucman, *The Hidden Wealth of Nations: The Scourge of Tax Havens*, University of Chicago Press, 2015, p. 40.

29 William Lazonick, 'The Functions of the Stock Market and the Fallacies of Shareholder Value', Institute for New Economic Thinking, Working Paper Series No. 58, June 2017.

30 Global Justice Now, '69 of the richest 100 entities on the planet are corporations, not governments, figures show', 17 October 2018.

31  Mordecai Kurz, 'On the Formation of Capital and Wealth: IT, Monopoly Power and Rising Inequality', SIEPR Working Paper No. 17–016, 25 June 2017.

32  Thomas Piketty, *Capital in the Twenty-First Century*, Harvard University Press, 2014.

33  Philip Mirowski and Rob Van Horn, 'The Rise of the Chicago School of Economics and the Birth of Neoliberalism', in Philip Mirowski and Dieter Plehwe (eds), *The Road From Mont Pelerin: The Making of the Neoliberal Thought Collective*, Harvard University Press, 2015, pp. 139–80.

34  Germán Gutiérrez and Thomas Philippon, 'The Failure of Free Entry', NBER Working Paper No. 26001, June 2019.

35  US Council of Economic Advisers, 'Benefits of Competition and Indicators of Market Power', Issue Brief, April 2016.

36  Leader article, 'The world's most valuable resource is no longer oil, but data', *The Economist*, 6 May 2017.

37  Diane Coyle, 'Practical competition policy implications of digital platforms', Bennett Institute for Public Policy Working Paper No. 01/2018, March 2018.

38  Matt Stoller, *Goliath: The 100-Year War Between Monopoly Power and Democracy*, Simon & Schuster, 2019, p. xviii.

## 2. This is your brain on shareholder value

1  See Extinction Rebellion, *This Is Not A Drill: An Extinction Rebellion Handbook*, Penguin, 2019.

2  See the paper 'Deep Adaptation: A Map for Navigating Climate Tragedy' by Jem Bendell, Professor of Sustainability Leadership at the University of Cumbria, 27 July 2018.

3  See the Climate Action Tracker, available at: https://climateaction-tracker.org/global/temperatures/ (accessed January 2020).

4  David Barstow, David Rohde and Stephanie Saul, 'Deep Water Horizon's Final Hours', *New York Times*, 25 December 2010.

5  Milton Friedman, 'The Social Responsibility of Business is to Increase its Profits', *New York Times Magazine*, 13 September 1970.

6  Friedman, 'The Social Responsibility of Business'.

7  Friedman, 'The Social Responsibility of Business'.

8  Daniel Stedman Jones, *Masters of the Universe: Hayek, Friedman, and the Birth of Neoliberal Politics*, Princeton University Press, 2012, p. 120.

9  Ronald Coase, 'The Nature of the Firm', *Economica*, 1937, Vol. 4, No. 16, 384–405.

10  United States v. Andreas, 216 F.3d 645 (7th. Cir. 2000).

11  Note by Damian Collins MP, Chair of the DCMS Committee: Summary of key issues from the Six4Three files. Available at: https://www.parliament.uk/documents/commons-committees/culture-media-and-sport/Note-by-Chair-and-selected-documents-ordered-from-Six4Three.pdf (accessed January 2020).

12  Roy Shapira and Luigi Zingales, 'Is Pollution Value-Maximizing? The DuPont Case', NBER Working Paper No. 23866, September 2017.

13  Felicity Lawrence, 'Asda slips up on banana price war', *The Guardian*, 12 October 2009.

14  George Stalk and Rob Lachenauer, *Hardball: Are you Playing to Play or Playing to Win?*, Harvard Business Review Press, 2004, cited by Steve Denning in 'The Origin Of "The World's Dumbest Idea": Milton Friedman', *Forbes*, 26 June 2013.

15  Ernst & Young, *Integrity in the spotlight: The future of compliance*, 15th Global Fraud Survey, 2018, p. 4. Visit the fraud surveys website at ey.com/fraudsurveys/global (accessed January 2020).

## 3. In big we trust

1  See Stephen Davis, Jon Lukomnik and David Pitt-Watson, *What They Do With Your Money: How the Financial System Fails Us, and How to Fix It*, Yale University Press, 2016.

2  Mark Sagoff, *The Economy of the Earth: Philosophy, Law, and the Environment*, 2nd edition, Cambridge University Press, 2008, quoted by

Ioannis Lianos in his paper 'Polycentric Competition Law', *Current Legal Problems*, 1 September 2018.

3  Adam Smith, *The Theory of Moral Sentiments*, Andrew Millar (London), 1759, p. 350.

4  Adam Smith, *The Wealth of Nations, Vol. I*, 1776. See Chapter II 'Of the Principle which Gives Occasion to the Division of Labour'.

5  Joseph Schumpeter, *Capitalism, Socialism, and Democracy*, Harper & Brothers, 1942.

6  US Supreme Court, Verizon Communications Inc. v. Trinko. Ruled on 13 January 2004.

7  See Jonathan B. Baker, 'Beyond Schumpeter vs. Arrow: How Antitrust Fosters Innovation', *Antitrust Law Journal*, 2007, Vol. 74, No. 3, 575–602; Carl Shapiro, 'Competition and Innovation: Did Arrow Hit the Bull's Eye?', in Josh Lerner and Scott Stern (eds), *The Rate and Direction of Inventive Activity Revisited*, NBER, 2012, pp. 361–404.

8  Mariana Mazzucato, *The Entrepreneurial State: Debunking Public vs. Private Sector Myths*, Penguin, 2018.

9  See Jonathan B. Baker, 'Taking the Error Out of "Error Cost" Analysis: What's Wrong with Antitrust's Right', *Antitrust Law Journal*, 2015, Vol. 80, No. 1, 1–38.

10  Zephyr Teachout and Lina Khan, 'Market Structure and Political Law: A Taxonomy of Power', *Duke Journal of Constitutional Law & Public Policy*, 2014, Vol. 9, No. 1, 37–74. See also Ioannis Lianos, 'Competition Law for the Digital Era: A Complex Systems Perspective', CLES Research Paper Series 6/2019, August 2019.

11  Adi Ayal, 'The Market for Bigness: Economic Power and Competition Agencies' Duty to Curtail it', *Journal of Antitrust Enforcement*, 2013, Vol. 1, No. 2, 221–46.

12  Charles Fishman, *The Wal-Mart Effect: How the World's Most Powerful Company Really Works—and How It's Transforming the American Economy*, Penguin, 2006, p. 2, cited in Teachout and Khan, 'Market Structure and Political Law'.

13  Global Justice Now, '69 of the richest 100 entities on the planet are corporations, not governments, figures show', 17 October 2018.

14 Uber Newsroom, 'Uber's Clean Air Plan to help London go electric', 23 October 2018.

15 James Maxwell and Forrest Briscoe, 'There's money in the air: the CFC ban and DuPont's regulatory strategy', *Business Strategy and the Environment*, 1997, Vol. 6, No. 5, 276–86.

16 Quoted in Justin Hyde, 'GM's "Engine Charlie" Wilson learned to live with a misquote', *Detroit Free Press*, 14 September 2008.

17 Kiran Stacey, 'Amazon and Microsoft unchallenged in $10bn "Jedi" contract review', *Financial Times*, 27 August 2019; Rana Foroohar, 'Government contracts become Amazon's new target market', *Financial Times*, 26 May 2019.

18 DealBook, 'Greenspan Calls to Break Up Banks "Too Big to Fail"', *New York Times*, 15 October 2009.

19 Alan Greenspan, 'Antitrust', paper given at the Antitrust Seminar of the National Association of Business Economists, Cleveland, Ohio, 25 September 1961.

20 Luigi Zingales, 'Towards a Political Theory of the Firm', *Journal of Economic Perspectives*, 2017, Vol. 31, No. 3, 113–30.

21 Katherine Smith et al., 'Corporate coalitions and policymaking in the European Union: How and why British American Tobacco promoted "Better Regulation"', *Journal of Health, Politics, Policy & Law*, 2015, Vol. 40, No. 2, 325–72.

22 https://influencemap.org/report/How-Big-Oil-Continues-to-Oppose-the-Paris-Agreement-38212275958aa21196dae3b76220bddc (accessed January 2020).

23 Greenpeace European Unit, *Smoke & Mirrors – How Europe's biggest polluters became their own regulators*, report published in March 2015.

24 See Teachout and Khan, 'Market Structure and Political Law', p. 47; Martin Gilens and Benjamin I. Page, 'Testing Theories of American Politics: Elites, Interest Groups, and Average Citizens', *Perspectives on Politics*, 2014, Vol. 12, No. 3, 564–81.

25 International Panel of Experts on Sustainable Food Systems, *Too Big to Feed: Exploring the impacts of mega-mergers, consolidation and concentration of power in the agri-food sector*, report published by IPES-Food, 2017.

26 The Lancet Commission, 'The Global Syndemic of Obesity, Under-nutrition, and Climate Change: *The Lancet* Commission report', *The Lancet*, 27 January 2019.

27 OECD, *Concentration in Seed Markets: Potential Effects and Policy Responses*, report published 4 December 2018.

28 Julia Carrie Wong, 'Facebook policy chief admits hiring PR firm to attack George Soros', *The Guardian*, 22 November 2018; Hannah Kuchler, 'Facebook accused of smearing George Soros', *Financial Times*, 15 November 2018.

29 See Mark Scott and Nicholas Hirst, 'Google's academic links under scrutiny', *Politico*, 13 May 2018; Adam Rogers, 'Looks Like Google Bought Favorable Research to Lobby With', *Wired*, 12 July 2017; Brody Mullins and Jack Nicas, 'Paying Professors: Inside Google's Academic Influence Campaign', *Wall Street Journal*, 14 July 2017.

30 Tom Hamburger and Matea Gold, 'Google, once disdainful of lobbying, now a master of Washington influence', *Washington Post*, 12 April 2014.

31 Kenneth P. Vogel, 'Google Critic Ousted From Think Tank Funded by the Tech Giant', *New York Times*, 30 August 2017.

32 Jonathan Tepper, 'Why Regulators Went Soft On Monopolies', *The American Conservative*, 9 January 2019.

33 Recode Staff, 'Full transcript: Senator Chuck Schumer on Recode Decode', *Recode Decode*, 13 March 2018.

34 Hal Singer, 'The Cambridge Affair Exposed Facebook's Dark Arts. Here's A Counterspell That Doesn't Kill Tech', *Forbes*, 2 April 2018.

35 For an overview of the documents visit: https://www.who.int/tobacco/media/en/TobaccoExplained.pdf; for the WHO response visit https://www.who.int/tobacco/dy_speeches1/en/ (websites accessed January 2020).

36 Nicholas Carr, *The Shallows: How the internet is changing the way we think, read and remember*, Atlantic Books, 2011.

37 Jesse Eisinger and Justin Elliott, 'These Professors Make More Than a Thousand Bucks an Hour Peddling Mega-Mergers', *ProPublica*, 16 November 2016.

38 Alexandra Stevenson, 'Facebook Admits It Was Used to Incite Violence in Myanmar', *New York Times*, 6 November 2018.

39 Ryan Gallagher, 'Twitter helped Chinese Government promote disinformation on repression of Uighurs', *The Intercept*, 19 August 2019.

40 Stephanie Kirchgaessner, 'Google loophole allows anti-abortion clinics to post deceptive ads', *The Guardian*, 19 August 2019.

41 James Landis, *The Administrative Process*, Yale University Press, 1938, p. 11.

42 Zingales, 'Towards a Political Theory of the Firm'.

43 Vicky Cann, 'Google: One of Brussels' most active lobbyists', *LobbyFacts.eu*, 12 December 2016.

44 Roy Shapira and Luigi Zingales, 'Is Pollution Value-Maximizing? The DuPont Case', NBER Working Paper No. 23866, September 2017.

45 Chad Bray, 'BP to Take $1.7 Billion Charge Over Deepwater Horizon Spill', *New York Times*, 16 January 2018.

46 Dina Srinivasan, 'The Antitrust Case Against Facebook', *Berkeley Business Law Journal*, 2019, Vol. 16, No. 1, 39–101.

47 Sarah E. Light, 'The Law of the Corporation as Environmental Law', *Stanford Law Review*, 2019, Vol. 71, 137–213; European Commission investigation, Case Number AT.40178 – Car Emissions.

48 Adam Ozanne, *Power and Neoclassical Economics: A Return to Political Economy in the Teaching of Economics*, Palgrave Macmillan, 2015, p. 85.

49 Robert B. Reich, *Saving Capitalism: For the Many, Not the Few*, Knopf, 2015, p. 11.

50 George Monbiot, 'Neoliberalism – the ideology at the root of all our problems', *The Guardian*, 15 April 2016.

## 4. Anti-what now?

1 Naomi R. Lamoreaux, *The Great Merger Movement in American Business, 1895–1904*, Cambridge University Press, 1985.

2  Richard Adelstein, 'The Last Autonomist', essay prepared for *Louis D. Brandeis 100: Then and Now*, celebrating the centennial of Brandeis' appointment to the Supreme Court, Brandeis University, 2016.

3  Michelle Meagher, 'Powerless Antitrust', *Competition Policy International*, 7 November 2019.

4  Herbert Hovenkamp, *Enterprise and American Law, 1836–1937*, Harvard University Press, 1991.

5  Martin J. Sklar, *The Corporate Reconstruction of American Capitalism, 1890–1916: The Market, the Law, and Politics*, Cambridge University Press, 1988.

6  Daniel A. Crane, 'The Dissociation of Incorporation and Regulation in the Progressive Era and the New Deal', in Naomi R. Lamoreaux and William J. Novak (eds), *Corporations and American Democracy*, Harvard University Press, 2017, pp. 109–38.

7  Louis D. Brandeis, 'A Curse of Bigness', *Harper's Weekly*, 10 January 1914.

8  Louis Brandeis, 'Shall We Abandon the Policy of Competition?' in Daniel A. Crane and Herbert Hovenkamp (eds), *The Making of Competition Policy*, Oxford University Press, 2013, Chapter 6.

9  Robert Van Horn, 'Jacob Viner's Critique of Chicago Neoliberalism' in Robert Van Horn, Philip Mirowski and Thomas A. Stapleford (eds), *Building Chicago Economics*, Cambridge University Press, 2011, Chapter 10.

10  Daniel Stedman Jones, *Masters of the Universe: Hayek, Friedman, and the Birth of Neoliberal Politics*, Princeton University Press, 2012, p. 97.

11  Daniel A. Crane, 'Antitrust and Democracy: A Case Study from German Fascism', *Law & Economics Working Papers*, 155, University of Michigan, published 17 April 2018.

12  Daniel Stedman Jones, *Masters of the Universe*, p. 36.

13  Friedrich Hayek, 'The Intellectuals and Socialism', *The University of Chicago Law Review*, 1949, Vol. 16, No. 3, 417–33.

14  Angus Burgin, *The Great Persuasion: Reinventing Free Markets since the Depression*, Harvard University Press, 2012.

15 Richard A. Posner, 'The Chicago School of Antitrust Analysis', *University of Pennsylvania Law Review*, 1979, Vol. 127, No. 4, 925–48.

16 Ioannis Lianos, 'Lost in Translation? Towards a Theory of Economic Transplants', *Current Legal Problems*, 2009, Vol. 62, No. 1, 346–404.

17 Sanjukta Paul, 'Antitrust As Allocator of Coordination Rights', *UCLA Law Review*, 2020, Vol. 67, No. 2, forthcoming.

18 Tim Wu, *The Curse of Bigness: Antitrust in the New Gilded Age*, Columbia Global Reports, 2018, p. 17.

19 Lina M. Khan, 'The Ideological Roots of America's Market Power Problem', *Yale Law Journal Forum*, 2018, Vol. 127, 960–79.

20 Barak Orbach, 'Was the Crisis in Antitrust a Trojan Horse?' *Antitrust Law Journal*, 2014, Vol. 79, No. 3, 881–902.

21 Mel Marquis and Brigitte Leucht, 'American Influences on EEC Competition Law: Two Paths, How Much Dependence?' in Kiran Patel and Heike Schweitzer (eds), *Historical Foundations of EU Competition Law*, Oxford University Press, 2013, pp. 125–61.

22 Mario Monti, former Competition Commissioner, 'The Future for Competition Policy in the European Union', speech at Merchant Taylors' Hall, London, 9 July 2001.

23 Joaquín Almunia, 'Competition and Consumers: The Future of EU Competition Policy', speech at European Competition Day, Madrid, 12 May 2010.

24 For the broader view, going back to the actual wording of the European Treaties, see Simon Holmes, 'Climate Change, Sustainability and Competition Law', draft article, 26 September 2019, available at: https://www.law.ox.ac.uk/sites/files/oxlaw/simon_holmes.pdf (accessed January 2020).

25 Anne C. Witt, *The More Economic Approach to EU Antitrust Law*, Hart Publishing, 2016; David J. Gerber, 'Two Forms of Modernization in European Competition Law', *Fordham International Law Journal*, 2008, Vol. 31, No. 5, 1235–65.

26 Suresh Naidu et al., 'Antitrust Remedies for Labor Market Power', *Harvard Law Review*, 2018, Vol. 132, 537–601.

27 Response sent by the Competition and Markets Authority to a letter from the Rt. Hon. Robert Halfon MP, dated 25 May 2018, available at: https://assets.publishing.service.gov.uk/media/5b1515b9e5274a1912717858/letter_to_robert_halfon.pdf (accessed January 2020).

28 Deepak Gupta and Lina Khan, 'Arbitration as Wealth Transfer', *Yale Law & Policy Review*, 2017, Vol. 35, No. 2, 499–520.

29 Sandeep Vaheesan, 'Accommodating Capital and Policing Labor: Antitrust in the Two Gilded Ages', *Maryland Law Review*, 2019, Vol. 78, No. 4, 766–827; Sanjukta Paul, 'The Enduring Ambiguities of Antitrust Liability for Worker Collective Action', *Loyola University Chicago Law Journal*, 2016, Vol. 47, 969–1048.

30 Marshall Steinbaum, 'Antitrust, the Gig Economy, and Labor Market Power', *Law & Contemporary Problems*, 2019, Vol. 82, No. 3, 45–64.

31 Maarten Pieter Schinkel and Yossi Spiegel, 'Can Collusion Promote Sustainable Consumption and Production?' *International Journal of Industrial Organization*, 2017, Vol. 53, 371–98.

32 Authority for Consumers & Markets, 'Industry-wide arrangements for the so-called Chicken of Tomorrow restrict competition', 26 January 2015.

33 See Rutger Claassen and Anna Gerbrandy, 'Rethinking European Competition Law: From a Consumer Welfare to a Capability Approach', *Utrecht Law Review*, 2016, Vol. 12, No. 1, 1–15; Julian Nowag, *Environmental Integration in Competition and Free Movement Laws*, Oxford University Press, 2016.

34 US Council of Economic Advisers, 'Benefits of Competition and Indicators of Market Power', Issue Brief, May 2016; Open Markets Institute, 'Monopoly by the Numbers', research available at https://openmarketsinstitute.org/explainer/monopoly-by-the-numbers/ (accessed January 2020).

35 Data collected by the Institute for Mergers, Acquisitions & Alliances, available at: https://imaa-institute.org/m-and-a-us-united-states/ (accessed January 2020).

36 Jonathan Tepper, *The Myth of Capitalism: Monopolies and the Death of Competition*, John Wiley & Sons, 2018, p. 163.

37 Hart-Scott-Rodino Annual Report, fiscal year 2015.

38 European Commission merger statistics, 21 September 1990 to 30 November 2019.

39 Digital Competition Expert Panel, *Unlocking digital competition*, report published March 2019.

40 Tim Wu, *The Curse of Bigness*, p. 123.

41 Lina M. Khan, 'Amazon's Antitrust Paradox', *Yale Law Journal*, 2017, Vol. 126, No. 3, 710–805.

42 Tommaso M. Valletti and Hans Zenger, 'Increasing Market Power and Merger Control', *Competition Law & Policy Debate*, 2019, Vol. 5, No. 1, 26–35.

43 Daniel Stedman Jones, *Masters of the Universe*, p. 32.

44 Daniel Stedman Jones, *Masters of the Universe*, p. 91.

45 Milton Friedman, 'Policy Forum: "Milton Friedman on business suicide"', *Cato Policy Report*, March/April 1999.

46 Norbert Wiener, *The Human Use Of Human Beings: Cybernetics and Society*, Avon Books edition, 1973, pp. 250–54.

## 5. Shareholders above the law

1 Weir v Secretary of State for Transport, example referenced in Paddy Ireland, 'Limited liability, shareholder rights and the problem of corporate irresponsibility', *Cambridge Journal of Economics*, 2010, Vol. 34, No. 5, 837–56.

2 Paddy Ireland, 'Limited liability'.

3 Daniel A. Crane, 'The Dissociation of Incorporation and Regulation in the Progressive Era and the New Deal', in Naomi R. Lamoreaux and William J. Novak (eds), *Corporations and American Democracy*, Harvard University Press, 2017, pp. 109–38.

4 Robert N. Anthony, 'The Trouble with Profit Maximization', *Harvard Business Review*, 1960, November-December, cited in Jeffrey N.

Gordon, 'The Rise of Independent Directors in the United States, 1950–2005: Of Shareholder Value and Stock Market Prices', *Stanford Law Review*, 2007, Vol. 59, 1465–1511.

5  Raymond C. Baumhart, 'How Ethical Are Businessmen?', *Harvard Business Review*, 1961, July-August, cited in Jeffrey N. Gordon, 'The Rise of Independent Directors'.

6  Colin Mayer, 'Reinventing the Corporation', *Journal of the British Academy*, 2016, Vol. 4, 53–72.

7  Steve Denning, 'The Origin Of "The World's Dumbest Idea": Milton Friedman', *Forbes*, 26 June 2013.

8  Transcript of Record, Dodge v. Ford Motor Co., 170 N.W. 668 (Mich. 1919) (No. 47) Cross-examination of Ford, at pages 213–30, cited in Linda Kawaguchi, 'Introduction to Dodge v. Ford Motor Co.: Primary Source and Commentary Material', *Chapman Law Review*, 2014, Vol. 17, No. 2, 493–578.

9  Dodge v. Ford Motor Co., 170 N.W. 668 (Mich. 1919).

10  See Robert J. Rhee, 'A Legal Theory of Shareholder Primacy', *Minnesota Law Review*, 2018, Vol. 102, 1951–2017.

11  eBay Domestic Holdings Inc. v. Newmark, 16 A.3d 1 (2010).

12  Harries v. The Church Commissioners for England [1992] 1 WLR 1241.

13  Section 172 of the Companies Act 2006.

14  Burwell v. Hobby Lobby Stores, Inc., 134 S. Ct. 2751 (2014).

15  Andrew R. Keay, 'The Public Enforcement of Directors' Duties', Working Paper, University of Leeds, School of Law, 16 January 2013.

16  See Robert J. Rhee, 'A Legal Theory of Shareholder Primacy'.

17  Lord Eldon LC in Carlen v. Drury (1812) 1 Vesey & Beames 154 at 158.

18  In Short v. Treasury Commissioners, 1948, the Court of Appeal stated that 'shareholders are not, in the eyes of the law, part owners of the company'.

19  Robert Monks, 'Corporate Governance: Past, Present, & Future', Harvard Law School Forum on Corporate Governance & Financial Regulation, posted on 4 March 2010.

20  Lynn A. Stout, 'The Shareholder Value Myth', *European Financial Review*, 30 April 2013.

21 John Kay, 'Shareholders think they own the company – they are wrong', *Financial Times*, 10 November 2015.

22 Colin Mayer, 'Reinventing the Corporation'.

23 William Lazonick, 'The Functions of the Stock Market and the Fallacies of Shareholder Value', Institute for New Economic Thinking, Working Paper Series No. 58, June 2017. See also Andrew G. Haldane, 'Who Owns A Company?', speech at the University of Edinburgh Corporate Finance Conference, 22 May 2015.

24 William Lazonick, 'The Functions of the Stock Market'.

25 For more on these 'agency costs' see Michael C. Jensen and William H. Meckling, 'Theory of the Firm: Managerial Behavior, agency costs and ownership structure', *Journal of Financial Economics*, 1976, Vol. 3, No. 4, 305–60.

26 Lynn A. Stout, 'The Shareholder Value Myth'.

27 Antony Page and Robert A. Katz, 'Freezing out Ben & Jerry: Corporate Law and the Sale of a Social Enterprise Icon', *Vermont Law Review*, 2012, Vol. 35, 211–50.

28 Antony Page and Robert A. Katz, 'Freezing out Ben & Jerry'.

29 Richard Dawkins, *The Selfish Gene*, Oxford University Press, 1976.

30 Ramsi Woodcock, 'The Antitrust Case for Consumer Primacy in Corporate Governance', *UC Irvine Law Review*, 2019, Vol. 10, forthcoming.

31 Leo E. Strine, 'The Dangers of Denial: The Need for a Clear-Eyed Understanding of the Power and Accountability Structure Established by the Delaware General Corporation Law', *Wake Forest Law Review*, 2015, Vol. 50, 761–71.

32 Edwin S. Rockefeller, *The Antitrust Religion*, Cato Institute, 2007.

33 Paul Krugman, 'Who Was Milton Friedman?', *New York Review of Books*, 15 February 2007.

## 6. A nation of shareholders

1 Margaret Thatcher, speech to Conservative Central Council, Felixstowe, 15 March 1986.

2  Edward N. Wolff, 'Household Wealth Trends in the United States, 1962 to 2016: Has Middle Class Wealth Recovered?', NBER Working Paper No. 24085, November 2017.

3  Edward N. Wolff, 'Household Wealth Trends'.

4  For a summary of the research see: https://www.sharesoc.org/ investor-academy/advanced-topics/uk-stock-market-statistics/ (accessed January 2020).

5  Paul Grout, William Megginson and Anna Zalewska, 'One Half-Billion Shareholders and Counting-Determinants of Individual Share Ownership Around the World', paper delivered at the 22nd Australasian Finance and Banking Conference, December 2009.

6  Julia Kollewe, 'Philip Green defends his record on BHS', *The Guardian*, 15 April 2018.

7  Commons Select Committee report, *Leadership failures and personal greed led to collapse of BHS*, published 25 July 2016.

8  Marc T. Moore, 'A Necessary Social Evil: The Indispensability of the Shareholder Value Corporation' (June 1, 2016). University of Cambridge Faculty of Law Research Paper No. 25, published June 2016.

9  See their website https://shareaction.org/about-us/ (accessed January 2020).

10 Tomorrow's Company, *Promoting long-term wealth: Reshaping corporate governance*, report for the All-party parliamentary Corporate Governance Group, APPG, 2017; Chris Flood, 'Value of global pension assets surges to $41.3tn', *Financial Times*, 5 February 2018.

11 Thomas Kochan, *Shaping the Future of Work: What Future Worker, Business, Government, and Education Leaders Need To Do For All To Prosper*, Business Expert Press, 2015, p. 19.

12 Mathew Lawrence, 'Corporate Governance Reform: Turning business towards long-term success', IPPR Commission on Economic Justice discussion paper, July 2017.

13 'Reward Work, Not Wealth', Oxfam briefing paper, January 2018.

14 William Lazonick, 'Labor in the Twenty-First Century: The Top 0.1% and the Disappearing Middle-Class', Institute for New Economic Thinking, Working Paper Series No. 4, 1 February 2015.

15 Justin Fox and Jay W. Lorsch, 'What Good Are Shareholders?', *Harvard Business Review*, 2012, July-August.

16 Jeffrey M. Jones, 'U.S. Stock Ownership Down Among All but Older, Higher-Income', *Gallup News*, 24 May 2017.

17 Transamerica Center for Retirement Studies, *Here and Now: How Women Can Take Control of Their Retirement*, survey report published 5 March 2018.

18 The National Center for Transgender Equality, quoted by Inequality.org, a project of the Institute for Policy Studies, in 'Economic Inequality Across Gender Diversity', available at: https://inequality.org/gender-inequality/ (accessed January 2020).

19 Judith Warner and Danielle Corley, 'The Women's Leadership Gap', *Center for American Progress*, 21 May 2017.

20 See Edward N. Wolff, 'Household Wealth Trends'; Edward N. Wolff, 'The Decline of African-American and Hispanic Wealth since the Great Recession', NBER Working Paper No. 25198, October 2018.

21 See Edward N. Wolff, 'Household Wealth Trends'.

22 William W. Bratton and Michael L. Wachter, 'Shareholder Primacy's Corporatist Origins: Adolf Berle and "The Modern Corporation"', *Journal of Corporation Law*, 2008, Vol. 34, No. 1, 99 and ff.

## 7. *Stakeholder antitrust*

1 Daniel A. Crane, 'The Dissociation of Incorporation and Regulation in the Progressive Era and the New Deal', in Naomi R. Lamoreaux and William J. Novak (eds), *Corporations and American Democracy*, Harvard University Press, 2017, pp. 109–38.

2 Robert Van Horn, 'Chicago's Shifting Attitude Toward Concentrations of Business Power (1934–1962)', *Seattle University Law Review*, 2011, Vol. 34, No. 4, 1527–44.

3 Rob Van Horn, 'Reinventing Monopoly and the Role of Corporations: The Roots of Chicago Law and Economics', in Philip

Mirowski and Dieter Plehwe (eds), *The Road From Mont Pelerin: The Making of the Neoliberal Thought Collective*, Harvard University Press, 2015, pp. 204–37.

4   Some scholars have explored this intersection. See Nell Abernathy, 'Rejecting the Theory of the Firm: Why the "Free-Market" Economy is a Myth and How to Rebuild Public Power', The Roosevelt Institute Issue Brief, 26 February 2019; Ramsi Woodcock, 'The Antitrust Case for Consumer Primacy in Corporate Governance', *UC Irvine Law Review*, 2019, Vol. 10, forthcoming; Florence Thépot, *The Interaction Between Competition Law and Corporate Governance: Opening the 'Black Box'*, Cambridge University Press, 2019; Sarah E. Light, 'The Law of the Corporation as Environmental Law', *Stanford Law Review*, 2019, Vol. 71, 137–213; Spencer Weber Waller, 'Corporate Governance and Competition Policy', *George Mason Law Review*, 2011, Vol. 18, No. 4, 833–87; Edward B. Rock, 'Corporate Law Through an Antitrust Lens', *Columbia Law Review*, 1992, Vol. 92, No. 3, 497–561; Daniel A. Crane, 'The Dissociation of Incorporation and Regulation'; Herbert Hovenkamp, *Enterprise and American Law, 1836–1937*, Harvard University Press, 1991.

## 8. *Speaking truth to market power*

1   For an overview of the (sometimes heated) debate, see John M. Newman, 'Anti-Hipster Antitrust', University of Miami School of Law, 16 September 2019.

2   Rutger Claassen and Anna Gerbrandy, 'Rethinking European Competition Law: From a Consumer Welfare to a Capability Approach', *Utrecht Law Review*, 2016, Vol. 12, No. 1, 1–15.

3   Ariel Ezrachi, 'Sponge', *Journal of Antitrust Enforcement*, 2017, Vol. 5, No. 1, 49–75.

4   See Article 3(3) of the Treaty on European Union, and Articles 7, 9, 11, and 101(3) of the Treaty on the Functioning of the European Union. See also Simon Holmes, 'Climate Change, Sustainability

and Competition Law', draft article, 26 September 2019, available at: https://www.law.ox.ac.uk/sites/files/oxlaw/simon_holmes.pdf (accessed January 2020).

5  See Gerhard Hofmann, 'Anchoring sustainability in competition', 15 June 2015, by the Forschungsgruppe Ethisch-Ökologisches Rating (the Ethical Ecological Rating Research Group), part of the Goethe University Frankfurt, available at: http://blog.ethisch-oekologisches-rating.org/nachhaltigkeit-im-wettbewerb-verankern/ (accessed January 2020).

6  See Adil Abdela, Kristina Karlsson and Marshall Steinbaum, 'Vertical integration and the Market Power Crisis', The Roosevelt Institute Issue Brief, April 2019; Jonathan B. Baker et al., 'Five Principles for Vertical Merger Enforcement Policy', *Georgetown Law Faculty Publications and Other Works*, April 2019, available at: https://scholarship.law.georgetown.edu/facpub/2148 (accessed January 2020).

7  Letter from the Rt. Hon. Lord Tyrie to the Secretary of State for Business, Energy & Industrial Strategy, dated 21 February 2019, available at: https://assets.publishing.service.gov.uk/government/uploads/system/uploads/attachment_data/file/781151/Letter_from_Andrew_Tyrie_to_the_Secretary_of_State_BEIS.pdf(accessed January 2020).

8  Zephyr Teachout and Lina Khan, 'Market Structure and Political Law: A Taxonomy of Power', *Duke Journal of Constitutional Law & Public Policy*, 2014, Vol. 9, No. 1, 37–74. See also Adam Ozanne, *Power and Neoclassical Economics: A Return to Political Economy in the Teaching of Economics*, Palgrave Macmillan, 2015.

9  European Commission, 'Communication on SMP guidelines', 26 April 2018, Paragraph 3.1 (58).

10  Allison Schrager, 'A Nobel-winning economist's guide to taming tech monopolies', *Quartz*, 27 June 2018.

11  Ioannis Lianos, 'The Principle of Effectiveness, Competition Law Remedies and the Limits of Adjudication', CLES Research Paper No. 6, published 10 August 2014.

12  Spencer Weber Waller, 'Antitrust and Democracy', Loyola University Chicago School of Law, 11 December 2017.

13  Elyse Dorsey, Jan Rybnicek and Joshua D. Wright, 'Hipster Antitrust Meets Public Choice Economics: The Consumer Welfare Standard, Rule of Law, and Rent-Seeking', *Competition Policy International*, 18 April 2018.

14  ProMarket blog, 'Restoring Antimonopoly Through Bright-Line Rules', Stigler Center at the University of Chicago Booth School of Business, posted 26 April 2019.

15  Robert Pitofsky, 'The Political Content of Antitrust', *University of Pennsylvania Law Review*, 1979, Vol. 127, No. 4, 1051–75.

16  Niamh Dunne, 'Commitment Decisions in EU Competition Law, *Journal of Competition Law and Economics*, 2014, Vol. 10, No. 2, 399–444.

17  Mark Zuckerberg, 'The Internet needs new rules. Let's start in these four areas', *Washington Post*, 30 March 2019.

18  Department for Business, Energy & Industrial Strategy, 'Corporate Governance Reform: The Government response to the green paper consultation', published August 2017.

19  State of California Department of Justice Press release, 'California Reaches Agreement with Tesoro to Protect Jobs and Monitor Gas Prices', 17 May 2013.

20  Federal Communications Commission, 'Applications of Comcast Corporation, General Electric Company and NBC Universal, Inc. for Consent to Assign Licenses and Transfer Control of Licensees', #FCC-11-4, 20 January 2011.

21  Peter Allen and Julie Henry, 'Revealed: how two boys blew whistle on the public school fees "cartel"', *The Telegraph*, 13 November 2005.

22  Office of Fair Trading, 'Schools: exchange of information on future fees', The National Archives No. CA98/05/2006, 20 November 2006.

23  Harry First and Eleanor M. Fox, 'Philadelphia National Bank, Globalization, and the Public Interest', *Antitrust Law Journal*, 2015, Vol. 80, No. 2, 307–52.

## 9. *Power to the people*

1   Herbert J. Hovenkamp, 'The Classical Corporation in American Legal Thought', *Georgetown Law Journal*, 1988, Vol. 76, No. 4, 1593–1690.

2   See Section 124A, 'Petition for winding up on the grounds of public interest', Insolvency Act 1986.

3   Ronald Coase, 'The Problem of Social Cost', *The Journal of Law & Economics*, 1960, Vol. III, October, 1–44.

4   Andrew G. Haldane, 'Who Owns A Company?', speech at the University of Edinburgh Corporate Finance Conference, 22 May 2015.

5   Nell Abernathy, 'Rejecting the Theory of the Firm: Why the "Free-Market" Economy is a Myth and How to Rebuild Public Power', The Roosevelt Institute Issue Brief, 26 February 2019.

6   Andrew Johnston, 'Governing Externalities: The Potential of Reflexive Corporate Social Responsibility', Centre for Business Research, University of Cambridge, Working Paper No. 436, September 2012.

7   Michael C. Jensen, 'Value maximization, stakeholder theory and the corporate objective function' in J. Andriof et al. (eds), *Unfolding Stakeholder Thinking*, Greenleaf Publishing, 2002, pp. 65–84.

8   Eric Lipton, 'Trump Rollbacks Target Offshore Rules "Written With Human Blood"', *New York Times*, 10 March 2018.

9   Rick Alexander, *Benefit Corporation Law and Governance: Pursuing Profit with Purpose*, Berrett-Koehler Publishers, 2017.

10  John Kenneth Galbraith, *American Capitalism: The concept of countervailing power*, Houghton Mifflin, 1952.

11  Anand Giridharadas, *Winners Take All: The Elite Charade of Changing the World*, Allen Lane, 2018.

12  https://www.pukkaherbs.com/our-mission/pukkas-mission-council/ (accessed January 2020).

13  https://www.divinechocolate.com/inside-divine (accessed January 2020).

14 https://www.aviva.com/social-purpose/good-governance/ (accessed January 2020).

15 https://www.toastale.com/equity-for-good/ (accessed January 2020).

16 https://cib.bnpparibas.com/sustain/danone-s-positive-incentive-financing-strategy_a-3-2238.html (accessed January 2020).

17 Sigurt Vitols, 'Prospects for trade unions in the evolving European system of corporate governance', European Trade Union Institute for Research, Education and Health and Safety, Brussels, November 2015, cited in Laurie Macfarlane, 'Why Wealth Is Determined More by Power Than Productivity', *Open Democracy*, 30 September 2018.

18 Gary Gorton and Frank A. Schmid, 'Capital, Labor, and the Firm: A Study of German Codetermination', *Journal of the European Economic Association*, 13 December 2010.

19 European Commission investigation case number AT.407178 – Car Emissions. See also Matthew Bodie, 'Worker participation, sustainability, and the puzzle of the Volkswagen emissions scandal', in Beate Sjåfjell and Christopher M. Bruner (eds), *Cambridge Handbook of Corporate Law, Corporate Governance and Sustainability*, Cambridge University Press, 2019, Chapter 18.

20 Kent Greenfield, 'Sticking the Landing: Making the Most of the "Stakeholder Moment"', *European Business Law Review*, 2015, Vol. 26, No. 1, 147–71.

21 See Christopher Zara, 'Coca-Cola Company (KO) Busted for "Greenwashing": PlantBottle Marketing Exaggerated Environmental Benefits, Says Consumer Report', *International Business Times*, 3 September 2013.

22 Serena Ng, 'Laundry Detergent from Jessica Alba's Honest Co. Contains Ingredient It Pledged to Avoid', *Wall Street Journal*, 10 March 2016.

23 Andrew R. Keay and Hao Zhang, 'An Analysis of Enlightened Shareholder Value in Light of Ex Post Opportunism and Incomplete Law', *European Company and Financial Law Review*, 2011, Vol. 8, No. 4, 445–75.

24 Mathew Lawrence, 'Corporate Governance Reform: Turning business towards long-term success', IPPR Commission on Economic Justice discussion paper, July 2017. Attorneys general have the power to bring what is called a *quo warranto* proceeding to challenge the actions of a corporation and most states have on their statute books a charter revocation law that allows for companies to be challenged in this way.

25 Andrew R. Keay, 'The Public Enforcement of Directors' Duties', Working Paper, University of Leeds, School of Law, 16 January 2013.

26 Andrew Jack and Leslie Hook, 'UK charities face scrutiny over ethics of investment policies', *Financial Times*, 4 March 2019.

27 See here for Audrey Tang's meetings archive: https://sayit.pdis.nat. gov.tw/speaker/audrey-tang-2 (accessed January 2020).

28 Joe Guinan and Martin O'Neill, 'From Community Wealth Building to System Change: Local Roots for Economic Transformation', *IPPR Progressive Review*, 2019, Vol. 25, No. 2, 382–92.

29 George Stigler, 'The Theory of Economic Regulation', *The Bell Journal of Economics and Management Science*, 1971, Vol. 2, No. 1, 3–21.

30 Germán Gutiérrez and Thomas Philippon, 'The Failure of Free Entry', NBER Working Paper No. 26001, June 2019.

31 Zephyr Teachout, 'Corporate Rules and Political Rules: Antitrust as Campaign Finance Reform', Fordham Law Legal Studies Research Paper No. 2384182, published 25 January 2014.

32 Digital Competition Expert Panel, *Unlocking digital competition*, report published March 2019, p. 5.

## Conclusion

1 Guy Singh-Watson, 'Can capitalism be responsible?', *Wicked Leeks*, 13 March 2019.

2 Guy Singh-Watson, 'Responsible capitalism: a manifesto', *Wicked Leeks*, 18 March 2019.

3  Jim Clifton, 'The Chairman's Blog: The World's Broken Workplace', *Gallup News*, 13 June 2017.

## Afterword

1  Kate Raworth, *Doughnut Economics: Seven Ways to Think Like a 21st-Century Economist*, Random House Business, 2017.
2  Simon Holmes, 'Climate Change, Sustainability and Competition Law', draft article, 26 September 2019, available at: https://www.law.ox.ac.uk/sites/files/oxlaw/simon_holmes.pdf (accessed January 2020).

# Acknowledgements

Although I conceived of this book in 2018, in fact these ideas had been five years or longer in the making already by then, as the preface describes. Perhaps this is why I have such a lot of people to thank for supporting me in my journey.

This being my first book, I really had no idea what I was doing when I set out to find a willing publisher. Mallory and Andrew Ladd shared their literary wisdom, and several other friends – especially Maria Nicholas and Tom Ebbutt – offered themselves as guinea pigs to read the initial book proposal.

I have not been short of people who have believed in the promise of this book and in my ability to write it: Kate Raworth gave generously of her time at a critical moment when I was about to give up; Rick Alexander has been unfailing in his enthusiasm for this project; James Perry helped me come up with the title; Kim Coupounas encouraged me to write the short paper that ballooned into a manuscript.

Numerous peers and colleagues, many of whom I have never had the opportunity to meet in person, gave me invaluable feedback on the manuscript or helped me to refine certain tricky points: Nina Boeger, David Coombs, Diane Coyle, Mike Hugman, Andrew Keay, Ioannis Lianos, Colin Mayer, Adam Ozanne, Hal Singer, Marshall Steinbaum, and Sandeep Vaheesan.

Harriet Brown, Hugo Foster and Simon Holmes read the whole thing cover to cover and their input can be seen in some big, and many small, changes that hopefully make the book more informative, more accurate and more enjoyable to read.

This book would not be worth reading but for the outstanding conceptual and editorial guidance I received from my agent,

Rebecca Carter at Janklow and Nesbit, and my editor, Lydia Yadi at Penguin Random House. They took a chance on this book, and I am hugely grateful.

I want to thank the British Library and SSRN – two totally free and absolutely essential resources for my research.

Writing a book is an enormous undertaking for anyone, but when you have two young kids it can be an overwhelming prospect. For that one year I missed a lot and slept only a little. Malachi and Indigo, my cheeky two, deleted precious files, scribbled on my notes, shrieked in the background whilst I was trying to gather my thoughts. But then, how lucky am I? I am swimming in love and my kids are my constant reminder that a book is just a book and not nearly as important as dancing in the kitchen.

My mother-in-law, Laura Meagher, deserves ultimate credit for urging me to seize the moment and get my ideas out there back when I was otherwise occupied with feeding and nappy changing. It seemed impossible then, and now it is done. She was right.

Also right, always, is Hayane Dahmen. She read proposals, she read manuscripts, but most critically she gave me the pep talks I needed, when I needed them, and coming from her they meant everything.

I want to thank Kresh: when all I could see was a wall, they helped me find a door. I want to thank the Flatties, School Girls and Lips Choir – I find that if I always do things that I think would make them proud then I cannot go far wrong.

My family is everything – my parents, Nawroze and Iqbal, and my siblings, Neil and Melissa – they know who I am, and no book will change that. It's a relief.

And finally to Dan. For once I have nothing to say because there is no way to thank you for steadying me from falling headlong into my own thoughts. Enjoy the quiet, it probably won't last long.

January 2020

# Appendix: Myths and realities

**Myth #1:** Free markets are competitive.

**Reality:** Free market competition creates power. In fact, 'competition' has come to be synonymous with domination and corporate power.

**Myth #2:** Companies compete by trying to best respond to the needs of society.

**Reality:** Companies compete for power, for the benefit of their shareholders, in ways that harm society.

**Myth #3:** Corporate power is benign.

**Reality:** There are many types of corporate power that allow the powerful to choose how to shape the economy and society in their interests.

**Myth #4:** We already control corporate power with antitrust.

**Reality:** Modern antitrust condones corporate power.

**Myth #5:** The law requires companies to maximize financial value for shareholders.

**Reality:** The law is being wilfully misinterpreted to our collective detriment as it does not require companies to maximize shareholder profit.

**Myth #6:** We are all shareholders; we all benefit from corporate focus on shareholders' interests.

**Reality:** Most shareholders are already wealthy.

# Glossary

I was challenged with providing a glossary for some of the more problematic words that appear in this book but for many of them their wide adoption has been driven, in part, by the fact that they have proven to be so malleable in meaning – the context, for these words, is everything, and meaning lies both with the writer and with the reader.

I was not sure I could attempt to pin down the definitions of these slippery words so I have landed on a compromise. I provide below a simplistic definition of some words, something that captures what *I* mean when I use the words in this book. But then, for those who want to know more and come to their own definitions, I have suggested some further sources. The list of further reading provided separately would also further inform the meanings of these words.

## Antitrust

This refers to the law and policy tools used to challenge corporate power.

The meaning of the word 'antitrust' has shifted over the last century and a half. Antitrust usually refers to the law – and enforcement of the law – that targets big business, following the enactment of the Sherman Act in 1890, but I use it to describe the containment of corporate power through other legal and policy tools as well (such as through corporate law).

In Europe and in most other jurisdictions in the world, this type of regulation is called 'competition law', or 'competition policy', as it concerns itself with the maintenance of competitive markets Competition law has a long history, predating the Sherman Act, with forms of competition law present in Roman law and in Medieval England. But most modern competition laws – and there are such laws on the statute books right across the world – are based on the US model.

I use 'antitrust' and 'competition law' interchangeably in this book – often preferring the former, as the word 'competition' is itself problematic (see definition of *Competition*).

See Chapter 4 for a brief history of antitrust, or for more detail see Tim Wu's *The Curse of Bigness: Antitrust in the New Gilded Age*, Matt Stoller's *Goliath: The 100-Year War Between Monopoly Power and Democracy* or my article 'Powerless Antitrust' (*Competition Policy International*, 7 November 2019).

## Chicago School

A school of economic thought based around *Neoclassical economics* and *Neoliberalism*.

## Competition

The rivalry between suppliers in the market as they strive to get customers to buy from them.

Chapter 1 explains why this word is so tricky, and how it has morphed from being used to describe the textbook paradigm of a market with many small sellers and buyers to increasingly being applied to concentrated markets with just a few big sellers or buyers.

For a technical discussion of the use of the word 'competition' for ideological purposes, see Sanjukta Paul's article,

'Antitrust As Allocator of Coordination Rights' (*UCLA Law Review*, 2020).

## Competition law

See *Antitrust*.

## Concentration

Market concentration relates to the number of economic players, companies or firms in a market and their relative market shares. A concentrated market is one in which a few companies have large market shares. An unconcentrated market is one in which there are many small players, each with low market share.

Market concentration is sometimes analysed using the 'concentration ratio'. For example, if a market has a four-firm concentration ratio of 80 per cent (or a CR4 of 80) then it means that the four largest firms have combined market shares of 80 per cent. An alternative measure of concentration is the Hirfindahl-Herschman Index (or HHI), which is calculated as the sum of the squares of the individual market shares of each firm in the market.

## Efficiency

This can refer to many different things. In economics, it is often used as a shorthand for 'Pareto efficiency', which describes an allocation of economic resources according to people's preferences under which no person could be made better off without making anyone else worse off.

'Pareto efficiency' is an umbrella term, under which sit specific aspects of efficiency such as 'allocative efficiency' (the right amount of resources are allocated to those who most want them) and 'productive efficiency' (the market produces things using the least possible resources).

Perfectly competitive markets are a necessary condition for 'Pareto efficiency' to arise.

As this book hopefully demonstrates, there are many things that matter to human welfare that are not captured by the simplistic economic concept of efficiency.

See any introductory economics textbook or Wikipedia for the basic definition, but see also Kate Raworth's *Doughnut Economics: Seven Ways to Think Like a 21st-Century Economist* or *Rethinking Economics: An Introduction to Pluralist Economics* for modern theories of economics that go well beyond the concept of 'efficiency'.

## Externalities

An externality – or 'spillover' – of a market transaction is an effect on third parties that derives from that transaction but which is not accounted for by the parties to that transaction (for example, the effect is not reflected in the market price). Externalities can be negative – such as pollution resulting from the burning of fossil fuels or the sale of a car (which is not factored into the price of the oil or of the car). Externalities can also be positive – such as the positive effect on society of an individual's decision to invest in their education. Economic theory predicts that the market will overproduce goods with negative externalities and underproduce goods with positive externalities.

# Monopoly

A company is said to hold a monopoly position in a market if they dominate the sale of goods or services in that market. Unlike a firm in a competitive market, a monopolist has the ability to raise prices and restrict output so that they can earn higher profits than under conditions of competition.

A pure monopoly is extremely rare – this would be the situation where there is a single seller and no competitors. Generally, a monopolist will still face some competitors, but the question is how much of a competitive restraint these other firms present for the pricing and output decisions of the monopolist. A market is treated as a *natural monopoly* when features of the industry require such a large scale of operations that the market will only accommodate a few firms.

Different legal systems have different thresholds for when a company is deemed to have a monopoly – it can be with a market share of 40 per cent in Europe or as high as 70 per cent in the US.

# Monopsony

This is the mirror image of *monopoly*. Whereas monopoly refers to the dominance of a seller in a product market – for example, the market for groceries – monopsony designates a firm with dominance as a buyer of inputs – for example, a grocery store may have monopsony power over farmers or food processors.

# Natural monopoly

See *Monopoly*.

## Neoclassical economics

A theory of economics that uses the concepts of supply and demand in the markets as the principal way of explaining how the economy works and why we end up with certain allocations of economic resources.

See also *Neoliberalism*.

## Neoliberalism

A political ideology that favours free markets, free trade, deregulation and privatization. It is premised on an understanding of economic actors as individualistic, self-interested, competitive, acquisitive and rational. It is the dominant ideology amongst policymakers and continues to shape much of public policy. It is based on a particular understanding of *Neoclassical economics*.

Neoliberalism was concocted in the 1940s by a group of academics through the foundation of an organization called the Mont Pelerin Society. The ideas were originally associated with the London School of Economics but eventually came to be championed by academics of the University of Chicago, which came to be known as the *Chicago School*.

For more on the evolution of neoliberalism, see Philip Mirowski and Dieter Plehwe's *The Road from Mont Pelerin* and Daniel Stedman Jones's *Masters of the Universe*.

## Oligopoly

This refers to the joint position of market dominance held by a small number of large firms representing significant combined market shares and market power.

## Shareholder value

Also known as 'shareholder value maximization' or 'shareholder primacy', this is the principle that the ultimate goal and measure of success for a company, and therefore the duty of its management, is the delivery of maximum financial returns to shareholders.

Shareholder value can be contrasted with *stakeholder value*, which is a term that implies that the purpose of corporations is to serve not just shareholders but other corporate stakeholders, such as workers, local communities, broader society and the environment.

## Stakeholder value

See *Shareholder value*.

# Further reading

*For more on the progressive antitrust agenda and the law and history of corporate governance and shareholder value, see the following resources.*

Nell Abernathy, 'Rejecting the Theory of the Firm: Why the "Free-Market" Economy is a Myth and How to Rebuild Public Power', The Roosevelt Institute Issue Brief, 26 February 2019.

Rick Alexander, *Benefit Corporation Law and Governance: Pursuing Profit with Purpose*, Berrett-Koehler Publishers, 2017.

Jonathan B. Baker, *The Antitrust Paradigm: Restoring a Competitive Economy*, Harvard University Press, 2019.

Jonathan B. Baker and Steven C. Salop, 'Antitrust, Competition Policy, and Inequality', *Georgetown Law Journal*, 2015, Vol. 104, No. 1, 1–28.

Ariel Ezrachi, 'Sponge', *Journal of Antitrust Enforcement*, 2017, Vol. 5, No. 1, 49–75.

Simon Holmes, 'Climate Change, Sustainability and Competition Law (Climate Change is an Existential Threat: Competition Law must be part of the solution and not part of the problem)', draft article, 26 September 2019, available at: https://www.law.ox.ac.uk/sites/files/oxlaw/simon_holmes.pdf (accessed January 2020).

Herbert Hovenkamp, *Enterprise and American Law, 1836–1937*, Harvard University Press, 1991.

Lina Khan and Sandeep Vaheesan, 'Market Power and Inequality: The Antitrust Counterrevolution and Its Discontents', *Harvard Law & Policy Review*, 2017, Vol. 11, 235–94.

Naomi R. Lamoreaux and William J. Novak (eds.), *Corporations and American Democracy*, Harvard University Press, 2017.

William Lazonick, 'The Functions of the Stock Market and the Fallacies of Shareholder Value', Institute for New Economic Thinking, Working Paper Series No. 58, June 2017.

Ioannis Lianos, 'Polycentric Competition Law', *Current Legal Problems*, 1 September 2018.

Barry C. Lynn, *Cornered: The New Monopoly Capitalism and the Economics of Destruction*, John Wiley & Sons, 2011.

David Millon, 'Radical Shareholder Primacy', *University of St. Thomas Law Journal*, 2013, Vol. 10, No. 4, 1013–44.

Philip Mirowski and Dieter Plehwe (eds), *The Road From Mont Pelerin: The Making of the Neoliberal Thought Collective*, Harvard University Press, 2015.

Lenore Palladino, 'Ending Shareholder Primacy in Corporate Governance', The Roosevelt Institute Issue Brief, 13 February 2019.

Sanjukta Paul, 'Antitrust As Allocator of Coordination Rights', *UCLA Law Review*, 2020, Vol. 67, No. 2, forthcoming.

Eric Posner and Glen Weyl, *Radical Markets: Uprooting Capitalism and Democracy for a Just Society*, Princeton University Press, 2018.

Daniel Stedman Jones, *Masters of the Universe: Hayek, Friedman, and the Birth of Neoliberal Politics*, Princeton University Press, 2012.

Marshall Steinbaum and Maurice E. Stucke, 'The Effective Competition Standard: A New Standard for Antitrust', The Roosevelt Institute Issue Brief, 25 September 2018.

Matt Stoller, *Goliath: The 100-Year War Between Monopoly Power and Democracy*, Simon & Schuster, 2019.

Lynn Stout, *The Shareholder Value Myth: How Putting Shareholders First Harms Investors, Corporations, and the Public*, Berrett-Koehler Publishers, 2012.

Zephyr Teachout, 'Corporate Rules and Political Rules: Antitrust as Campaign Finance Reform', Fordham Law Legal Studies Research Paper No. 2384182, published 25 January 2014.

Zephyr Teachout and Lina Khan, 'Market Structure and Political Law: A Taxonomy of Power, *Duke Journal of Constitutional Law & Public Policy*, 2014, Vol. 9, No. 1, 37–74.

Jonathan Tepper with Denise Hearn, *The Myth of Capitalism: Monopolies and the Death of Competition*, John Wiley & Sons, 2018.

Christopher Townley, 'Is There (Still) Room for Non-Economic Arguments in Article 101 TFEU Cases?' in Caroline Heide-Jørgensen (ed.), *Aims and Values in Competition Law*, Djøf Publishing, 2013.

Elizabeth Warren, 'Empowering American Workers and Raising Wages', 3 October 2019, available at: https://medium.com/@team-warren/empowering-american-workers-and-raising-wages-a60f278 47bcb (accessed January 2020).

Elizabeth Warren, 'Here's how we can break up Big Tech', 8 March 2019, available at: https://medium.com/@teamwarren/heres-how-we-can-break-up-big-tech-9ad9e0da324c (accessed January 2020).

Elizabeth Warren, 'Companies Shouldn't Be Accountable Only to Shareholders', *Wall Street Journal*, 14 August 2018.

Tim Wu, *The Curse of Bigness: Antitrust in the New Gilded Age*, Columbia Global Reports, 2018.

*For more on breaking with mainstream thinking in economics and public policy, see the following resources.*

Liliann Fischer et al. (eds), *Rethinking Economics: An Introduction to Pluralist Economics*, Routledge, 2017.

David Graeber, *Debt: The First 5000 Years*, Melville House Publishing, 2nd edition, 2014.

Tim Jackson, *Prosperity Without Growth*, Routledge, 2nd edition, 2016.

Owen Jones, *The Establishment: And How They Get Away with It*, Penguin, 2015.

Katrine Marçal, *Who Cooked Adam Smith's Dinner?: A Story About Women and Economics* (translated from the original Swedish in 2014), Portobello Books, 2015.

Mariana Mazzucato, *The Entrepreneurial State: Debunking Public vs. Private Sector Myths*, revised edition, Penguin, 2018.

Adam Ozanne, *Power and Neoclassical Economics: A Return to Political Economy in the Teaching of Economics*, Palgrave Macmillan, 2015.

Kate Raworth, *Doughnut Economics: Seven Ways to Think Like a 21st-Century Economist*, Random House Business, 2017.

E. F. Schumacher, *Small is Beautiful: A Study of Economics as if People Mattered* (first published in 1973), HarperCollins, 2010.

George R. Stewart, *Earth Abides* (first published in 1949), Gollancz, 1999.

# Index

# Index

# PENGUIN PARTNERSHIPS

Penguin Partnerships is the Creative Sales and Promotions team at Penguin Random House. We have a long history of working with clients on a wide variety of briefs, specializing in brand promotions, bespoke publishing and retail exclusives, plus corporate, entertainment and media partnerships.

We can respond quickly to briefs and specialize in repurposing books and content for sales promotions, for use as incentives and retail exclusives as well as creating content for new books in collaboration with our partners as part of branded book relationships.

Equally if you'd simply like to buy a bulk quantity of one of our existing books at a special discount, we can help with that too. Our books can make excellent corporate or employee gifts.

Special editions, including personalized covers, excerpts of existing books or books with corporate logos can be created in large quantities for special needs.

We can work within your budget to deliver whatever you want, however you want it.

**For more information, please contact**
**salesenquiries@penguinrandomhouse.co.uk**